THERE IS NO SUCH THING AS A FREE PRESS

...and we need one more than ever

MICK HUME

SOCIETAS
essays in political
& cultural criticism

imprint-academic.com

Copyright © Mick Hume, 2012

The moral rights of the author have been asserted.
No part of this publication may be reproduced in any form
without permission, except for the quotation of brief passages
in criticism and discussion.

Published in the UK by
Imprint Academic, PO Box 200, Exeter EX5 5YX, UK

Distributed in the USA by
Ingram Book Company,
One Ingram Blvd., La Vergne, TN 37086, USA

ISBN 9781845403508

A CIP catalogue record for this book is available from the
British Library and US Library of Congress

For Ginny, my wife,
a model of true tolerance

Contents

Preface   v

Chapter One: "I Believe in a Free Press, But..."   1

Chapter Two: Whose Ethics Are They Anyway?   27

Chapter Three: Fear and Loathing of the Popular   58

Chapter Four: Why Blame "the Meejah"?   87

Chapter Five: Here is the News: Journalism as Narcissism   112

Chapter Six: Leveson's Mission—Purging the Press   140

Chapter Seven: Manifesto for a Free Press   173

Preface

This short book is partly about the problems within the UK press. But it is principally about problems with the way we view the press today. It has been written to challenge some distorted perceptions about the role of the media that are as confused as they are widely-shared.

My main concern is that a proper belief in the freedom of the press has gone out of fashion. Lord Justice Leveson's Inquiry into the "culture, practice and ethics" of the British media did not start these corrosive trends. But it gave them the stamp of official approval. As argued in the pages that follow, that judicial probe into the phone-hacking scandal at the late *News of the World* has been a pretext for a mission to purge the entire "popular" press, using high-profile victims as human shields, high-ranking celebrities as voice-over artists, and high-minded talk of "ethics" as a code for advancing an elitist political and cultural agenda.

Any doubt as to which way the wind might be blowing was pretty well dispelled as I was finishing the book, when it was reported that Lord Justice Leveson had phoned the government's top official to demand that Tory education secretary Michael Gove be "gagged", after the minister had the temerity to point out that the Leveson Inquiry was having a "chilling" effect on the press.[1] There are limits to freedom of expression for such heresies these days.

The aim of the book is to turn most of the widespread assumptions about the media on their head. To argue that, far from needing more regulation and regimentation, what the press needs is greater freedom and openness. And to show how, while everybody pays lip service to the importance of press freedom, in the real world it is being muffled under a chokehold of conformism.

Writing such a book has involved me dealing with some strange problems. I am a man of the Left who cut his journalistic teeth writing for and editing revolutionary newspapers and magazines. In the course of that career as a polemicist and propagandist (no, it doesn't mean liar, look it up), I have expended countless words criticising the "bourgeois" press, not least the tabloids, and might in the past have endorsed the traditional Left view that the press is only truly free for those who own it. I still find much of what is in the tabloid press not to my taste, though I admire their smart columnists and sharp sub-editing.

Yet in the atmosphere of today, when fundamental principles are at stake in the attempt to purge the press, I find myself far more concerned to defend freedom for the demonised tabloids—and their much-maligned readers—against the cultural elites who seem to think that "popular" is a dirty word and that press freedom is not an indivisible right, but a privilege to be doled out only to the deserving.

The strangest thing is that media liberals, political Leftists and civil liberties lobbyists have become some of the main players pursuing the crusade for firmer regulation and the "ethical" cleansing of the press. Many have effectively deserted the cause of liberty and gone over to the other side in the culture war over press freedom. That is why, instead of wasting time joining in the attack on the tabloids, these are the targets against which I often hit hardest here.

The other revealing news received just as I finished the book was a statement from the long-established Campaign for Press and Broadcasting Freedom, calling for the post-Leveson reforms to lead to a new regulatory regime to be "established by statute".[2] In other words, by the legal power of the state. Call me old fashioned, but I suspect the idea that campaigning for press freedom could mean demanding state-backed supervision might be news to those who fought for centuries to free the press in Britain from controls and regulations "established by statute" or by order of the Crown.

There are serious problems with the press. None of them are going to be solved by tighter regulation and a purge that can only make worse the absence of freedom, open-mindedness and plurality in the UK press today.

These developments come at a time when, in the midst of a social and economic crisis and the demise of the old politics, a free press has potentially become more important than ever. A crisis is not only supposed to mean a situation in which things get worse and worse. It means a crossroads, a time for decisions —in this case, about which way we want our society, politics and economy to go. There has been too little serious discussion in the UK or the West about such options or alternatives. This is where a free and open press, in all of its forms, could have a role to play in constructing a future.

Once, in the dim mists of history, an emerging free press became the focus of new democratic movements in the eighteenth and nineteenth centuries. As the young Karl Marx described it in his first newspaper articles arguing against Prussian state censorship in the 1840s, a free press was seen as "the embodiment of a people's faith in itself, the eloquent link that connects the individual with the state and the world, the embodied culture that transforms material struggles into intellectual struggles".[3] That brief flowering of a free press as a champion of humanity and herald of change did not last long.

Now we are witnessing the exhaustion and hollowing out of the old moribund politics across the West. In the absence of other outlets, the media has become the sole venue for political life. There is surely an opportunity for a flowering of a free press once more, particularly via the internet, to host an argument about new visions and alternative outlooks.

Which is why, despite the fact that this book is not short of criticism, I am not at all negative about the prospects for the press. My concern is that an opportunity for a fresh era of a free press is at risk of being wasted.

We are talking here about the press in all its shapes and forms, not just the traditional newspapers. The "press" has been a generic term for anything published since the introduction of the original printing press to England in the fifteenth century. It is a very long time since anything was printed using that historic method, yet the label has persisted. In the same spirit I use it here to defend freedom for the press in all of its published varieties, from the world of print to the internet, where the future of press freedom surely belongs.

This book is not, however, really about the economic crisis and financial pressures facing the press and journalism today. We all know those problems exist, and they are beyond the scope of this argument. What is certain is that so long as people want news, entertainment and opinions the press will survive in some, perhaps many, forms. What matters is that journalism survives into the new age of the press as a serious, free, open and diverse form of communication. Whether newspapers are distributed for free or charge for online content in their struggle for economic survival, the important thing is that the press does not give away or sell its freedom in the process.

While the focus of my argument is on the debate over press freedom in the UK that has come into sharp focus around the Leveson Inquiry, the trends discussed are also an international phenomenon. The Finkelstein Report into the future of press regulation in Australia has gone beyond the ideas discussed at Leveson, to propose the state as watchdog of the press. And even in the USA, home of the First Amendment commitment to freedom of speech and a free press, the mood has been turning against unbridled freedom of expression from Congress to the college campus.

The case for press freedom presented here flows from years of argument as a political journalist and propagandist in both the alternative and mainstream media. In 1988 I was the launch editor of *Living Marxism* magazine, relaunched as the taboo-busting *LM* magazine in the nineties and forced to close in 2000 after being sued under England's atrocious libel laws. Then I became the launch editor of *Spiked* (spiked-online.com), the UK's first and best web-based current affairs and comment magazine, of which I am now editor-at-large. I have also been privileged to write many articles for *The Times* (London), which is of course owned by News Corp and therefore Rupert Murdoch. I was a libertarian Marxist columnist at *The Times* for almost 10 years, having first been recruited by the then-comment editor—Michael Gove. Murdochphobics and conspiracy mongers can make of that what they will.

These arguments would not, however, have been possible without the input of others. I would like to recognise and thank my overworked and underpaid colleagues at *Spiked*, where many of these ideas were first aired and developed—a magazine that is the living proof of the potential for a new online media today. Particular thanks to Brendan O'Neill, the *Spiked* editor, a fighter for freedom of expression and critic of conformism who is not afraid to be in a minority of one when he believes *Spiked* is right. Special thanks are also due to Professor Frank Furedi, a source of the most inspiring ideas and sound advice (not all of which I have taken) for the past 30 years. The responsibility for the text, warts and all, is of course mine alone.

In the face of all the "ethical" attacks on the alleged cultural crimes of the mass media and the popular press today, I think back again to what my old friend Karl Marx said in his youthful defence of press freedom against Prussian state censorship, 170 years ago. Amid high-level talk of the dangers of allowing the press to run free, Marx was adamant that "lack of freedom is the real mortal danger for mankind". To those who warned of the damage the reckless, immoral elements of a free press might do, the young newspaper columnist was equally unsympathetic: "[L]eaving aside the moral consequences, bear in mind that you cannot enjoy the advantages of a free press without putting up with its inconveniences. You cannot pluck the rose without its thorns! And what do you lose with a free press?"[4]

To surrender the rose of a free and open press to the conformists, regulators and inquisitors, on the other hand, because you are scared of those inconvenient tabloid thorns, is to risk losing everything.

Mick Hume
London, July 2012

www.freethepress.co.uk
Email: mick.hume@freethepress.co.uk

1   *Mail on Sunday*, 17 June 2012.
2   Campaign for Press and Broadcasting Freedom, *Evidence to the Leveson Inquiry*, 11 July 2012 (http://www.cpbf.org.uk/body.php?Subject=Leveson%20Inquiry&doctype=news&id=2748).
3   Karl Marx, 'On freedom of the press', *Rheinische Zeitung*, No 135, Supplement, 15 May 1842 (http://www.marxists.org/archive/marx/works/1842/free-press/ch05.htm).
4   *Ibid.*

Chapter One

"I Believe in a Free Press, But..."

Milne: No matter how imperfect things are, if you've got a free press everything is correctable, and without it everything is concealable.

Ruth: I'm with you on the free press. It's the newspapers I can't stand.

— Tom Stoppard, *Night and Day* (1978), Act 1.

Everybody in British public life claims to believe in freedom of expression and a free press. Strange, then, that so many of them should now choose to exercise that freedom in order to declare that it should be limited — at least for others.

The mantra of the moment, which became the plea of many witnesses at Lord Justice Leveson's inquiry into the British press, is; "Of course I believe in a free press, BUT..." And the "buts" are getting bigger.

"But", they insist, there must be tougher press regulation. "But" we need more protection of privacy. "But" journalists should be licensed professionals. "But" the media should only publish a story if it's in the Public Interest. "But" Page 3 pin-ups must be banned. "But" snooping tabloid reporters should be treated more or less like paedophiles. "But" the world of news would be a better place if more tawdry papers went the way of the deceased *News of the World*...

What's more, the expanding "buts" now stretch way beyond the world of the media, to blaming the abuse of press freedom for manifold problems in British society. Yes, we are told, a free press is important; "but" the press has to be reined in now as punishment for the way that it has corrupted our politics and policing, our women and children, and even our religion, football.

The ever-broader "buts" being attached to support for press freedom confirm that the life-crisis facing the press today is about much more than specific crimes such as phone-hacking. Those problems have become the pretext to start hacking away at bigger questions about the media and society. As the Leveson Inquiry's brief from prime minister David Cameron made clear, it was set up not merely to investigate the phone-hacking scandal — the police were already doing that on a grand scale — but to interrogate and propose changes to the entire "culture, practice and ethics" of the media. It seems improbable that the government expected the Inquiry to conclude that what the press — and particularly the popular press — needs now is greater liberty.

In his opening statement at the start of the Inquiry's formal hearings in November 2011, Lord Justice Leveson set the tone for what was to come by making clear his own membership of the "I believe in press freedom, but…" club. Leveson conceded that freedom of the press was "fundamental" to "our way of life", and generously insisted that he had "no wish to stifle freedom of speech or expression", before immediately adding the obligatory "But". In his case it was, "But I anticipate that monitoring will take place of press coverage [of the Inquiry] and it might be appropriate to conclude that these vital rights are being abused, which itself would provide evidence of culture, practice and ethics which would could [sic] be relevant to my ultimate recommendations". The implication appeared to be that the press can enjoy its "vital rights" so long as it does not "abuse" them by saying the wrong thing. The media is "free" to remain on-message and to be monitored.[1]

Let me, then, try to enter into the spirit of the age. Of course, I too believe in free speech and a free press. I agree that there is much to dislike in the British press. BUT I also believe that freedom is inevitably a messy business. It is not a privilege to be handed out only to those who meet your moral standards. The fact that some journalists and publications might choose to misuse and even "abuse" their "vital rights" is no reason to try to limit or restrain the right to freedom of expression. To seek to sanitise freedom is to risk killing it. A "bad", "toxic" and "unethical" press that is free will always be better than a "good", "clean" and "pure" press that is unfree, if we want to stand a chance of getting close to the truth. But me no buts about a free press, please.

Press freedom is not some fluffy but impractical ideal, like "free love", to be butted out of existence by those who disapprove of its consequences. Freedom of expression is not an empty slogan to play lip service to, like motherhood, apple pie, European Union or the Big Society. It is a hard-won historic right that helped to pave the way for the creation of the modern democratic world. Free speech is the fundamental bedrock liberty of our society.

Without the freedom to think, say, write, publish, read, hear, love and hate what we choose, other freedoms would be impossible to imagine. The Enlightenment that brought us into the modern age of reason and rational thought, of science and the arts, was only possible because of the struggle for the freedom of the press that went alongside it. Freedom of expression remains the only hope we have of knowing anything. It is how society conducts its debates between clashing opinions and makes its decisions about what it believes to be right and true. A free press, in all of its forms, is the lifeblood of a free society and a vital citizenry.

That is why the suppression of a free press has always been the early hallmark of dictatorship. And it is why the flowering of an independent press has often been a sign that democratic change is on the way, from the radical newssheets of eighteenth and nineteenth century Europe and America to the blogs and online publications that break out at times of upheaval in the developing world today.

So yes, I believe absolutely in the principle of a free press. And yes, it is clear that the exercise of that freedom can cause plenty of trouble for people. Nobody should be naïve or complacent about the problems of journalistic standards today. Nor should we try to take a morally neutral view of an irresponsible press.

BUT the far more important point is that freedom of expression is always a messy affair. It means allowing others the freedom to publish things that we may not want to see. As George Orwell put it in his 1945 essay on "The Freedom of the Press", written as an (ironically unpublished) preface to *Animal Farm*, "If liberty means anything at all it means the right to tell people what they do not want to hear".[2]

A free press must mean one that is free, not from being judged or subjected to the normal criminal law, but from being restrained or punished on the grounds of taste or "decency" or offended feelings or outraged sensibilities. The misuse of our freedom by some is not an excuse for allowing the authorities to misappropriate it.

However you or I might wish it to be, the hard truth is that a free press does not have to conform to our or anybody else's notions of what is good journalism, or of what is ethical to report, or of what is too offensive to say or show. The principle of press freedom might look pristine when set down on paper. But in reality that lofty principle can be exploited for low purposes. Freedom is indeed a muddy and sometimes bloody business.

It might come as a shock to a few more naïve souls. But the truth is that not everybody who chooses to write for a newspaper, or to rant on the web, or in other ways to say something in public, will have the piety of Jesus Christ, the wisdom of Socrates or the purity of soul of Hugh Grant or Max Mosley. Nor should they be expected to. There is no requirement to pass a morality test in order to earn the right to free expression. Contrary to the cliché of contemporary prejudice, your inalienable rights are not dependent upon the fulfilment of what somebody else claims are your responsibilities.

Looking down on the seething mass of hacks and readers from the mock-ivory towers of journalism academia, some would like to impose a standard of almost saintly virtue on the common trade. Two American professors of journalism, for example, have declared investigative journalists to be our society's "Custodians of Conscience" and defenders of "Public Virtue".[3]

A nice thought with which to inspire the students, no doubt. Back down on Grub Street, however, not every journalist is possessed by a sense of public duty. Not all want to or can be held to the standards that would be imposed by others. Indeed the question of what are acceptable standards of good journalism is not something that can be declared in advance or settled for all time. Hopefully many journalists will take their work and themselves seriously enough. Hopefully the public will hold journalists to account for what they say and judge them accordingly. Those hopes, however, are not reasons or excuses to seek to limit the right to free expression for those who fail to fulfil the dream of a press fit for Messrs Grant and Mosley to read or appear in.

Yet today the "I believe in press freedom, but..." lobby appears to take a very different view of freedom of expression. They demand that rights be granted only with responsibilities. They insist on the need for "ethical" journalism. They declare that a clear line must be drawn, in the moral sand, the press regulations and possibly the law, between journalism which is pursuing serious and important issues "in the public interest", and that which is merely peddling stories which interest the public.

In the words of Deputy Assistant Commissioner Sue Akers of the Metropolitan Police, appearing before the Leveson Inquiry, the trouble with the tabloids is not just that they have employed dubious methods to obtain information, but have done so merely to publish "stories which I would describe as salacious gossip, not what I would describe as being remotely in the public interest".[4] The notion of a senior police officer issuing guidelines on what sort of news is fit for the press to publish is not one we might normally associate with a healthy democracy. In the other-worldly atmosphere created around the phone-hacking scandal and the Leveson Inquiry, however, the idea of a top cop defining "the public interest" as part of the attempt to police the motives and minds of tabloid journalists—and their readers—can now pass for normal.

The attempt to draw an ethical line between journalism that deserves to be free and "so-called" journalism that does not has reached new heights around the Leveson Inquiry into the British media. Whatever shape the new system of press regul-ation eventually takes, the tabloids have already been found guilty not only of crimes against "ethical public interest journal-ism", but of inhumanity. This should perhaps not be too sur-prising as there appears to be a quite widespread view among the literati, luvvies and tweeters that tabloid journalists and editors are not really human at all, and hence undeserving of the human right to free expression.

Tabloid reporters are, according to one writer from the *Independent* giving evidence at Leveson, "a different breed" from quality journalists such as her. Hugh Grant told the Inquiry that Britain's tabloids had nurtured "a culture of pure evil". Comedian Steve Coogan said some tabloid hacks were "sociopaths" inhabiting "an amoral universe". Writer Will Self described a former *NotW* journalist who appeared at the Inquiry as exhibiting "a feral, rat-like persona". A professor of journ-alism observed that "a more off-putting example of the species it would be hard to imagine". One fancied it was not the human species she had in mind. A former editor of BBC radio's flagship *Today* programme declared that "the tabloid press is peopled by beings who are not like us". Meanwhile the enlightened modern class of Twitter and Facebook users acted as backing chorus for Leveson, holding forth for months on the merits of "inhuman" tabloid "scum" and "animals".[5]

In the 1980s, I recall, ITV's satirical puppet show *Spitting Image* depicted tabloid reporters as pigs dressed in dirty rain-

coats and trilbies. Ben Elton did a comedy routine which suggested Dante had been wrong because at the very bottom of the
deepest circle of Hell there lay a lower depth occupied by "the
bloke who edits the *Sun*". These hilarious jokes now seem to
have become the intellectual basis of an intelligentsia consensus.

In short, the sort of language traditionally used by tabloids
to pursue their favourite targets—paedophiles, welfare scroun-
gers, England football managers—is now being deployed
against them by serious journalists in support of the Leveson
Inquiry and the demand for tighter regulation. You might consider that a delicious irony. Or you might call it an unpalatable
display of double standards. Either way, it is not the last time
we will note the anti-tabloid brigade using tactics that they
condemn in others.

The contention of this book is that freedom of the press, like
all meaningful freedoms, is not divisible. You cannot say that
you abolish slavery, but then do so only for white people or
Christians. Similarly you cannot declare your support for a free
press, but only defend freedom for those parts of it that meet
your chosen standards, however high-minded those motives
might appear.

Freedom of expression is not to be rationed out like charity,
to only the most "deserving" cases. A right is a right, and is not
limited by any incumbent responsibilities. Of course any good
journalist should be prepared to stand up and take responsibility for what they write, and for the methods they use to get
that story. But the wish to see responsible journalism cannot be
used to trample on the freedom of others.

The messy affair of press freedom does not fit easily into
pristine and pre-conceived notions of "ethical journalism" and
"the public interest". Before asking some questions about what
such slogans might really mean today, it might be worth trying
to put matters in some perspective by stepping out of the
present febrile atmosphere of "buts" and demands for ethics
and ombudsmen.

Let us take a step back to a time when those demanding a
free press, or publishing what was deemed to be offensive in

Britain, could expect an invitation, not to attend Lord Justice Leveson's genteel inquiry at the Royal Courts of Justice for a couple of hours, but to attend a cell in the Tower of London for somewhat longer.

A question that occurs to me, listening to our present-day crusaders for ethical journalism who want to "but" press freedom into respectability, and who appear to cheer the downfall, arrest and prosecution of "rogue" and "rat-like" journalists, is this: what on earth would they have made of John Wilkes, the eighteenth century champion of press freedom who fought for the liberty to offend every standard of civilised society in his time?

"Wilkes and Liberty!"

John Wilkes (1725–1797) was a Member of Parliament and Lord Mayor of London, famed as a great hero of the history-making struggle for rights and a free press in England. At a time when any criticism of the Crown and its ministers could still get you locked up for "seditious libel", Wilkes published a newspaper whose first edition declared to an intolerant King and government that "the liberty of the press" was "the birthright of every Briton". A little-noticed statue of Wilkes stands in the City of London today, the inscription on which rightly hails him as "A champion of English freedom".

A maverick early journalist, editor and publisher as well as an MP, Wilkes is remembered as a key figure in the emergence of radical democratic politics in England and beyond. Between 1763 and 1774 Wilkes and his sharpened pen fought running political battles with governments of the autocratic Court Party that acted as lickspittles for King George III. When he was locked up as a result, huge crowds of his supporters fought actual battles through the streets of London with the authorities and anybody who opposed their champion. The "Wilkes riots" were one of first great demonstrations of the popular will in British politics, as those whom Wilkes called "the middling and inferior set of people" made themselves both heard and forcibly felt, and the cry "Wilkes and Liberty!" became the slogan of the emerging movement for political reform.

In the course of a long political struggle that began over his insistence on press freedom, Wilkes won hard-fought and historic victories over the state's use of "general warrants" to arrest political opponents, for the right of electors to choose the MP they wanted and, most importantly for our argument here, for the freedom to report the proceedings of parliament in newspapers. For publishing what the authorities did not like he was convicted of seditious libel, had his house ransacked and was sent to the Tower of London by order of the government; was sentenced to almost two years in prison, declared an "outlaw" in England, expelled from parliament and then barred from returning there despite winning four elections; and, among other injuries, shot in the groin by an outraged enemy. Meanwhile a constant stream of insults and invective poured on to Wilkes' head from high places, his enemies spanning the Establishment from the Crown downwards. Through all this he stood as rock steady as his statue for the freedom of the press.

Such was John Wilkes, the hero of English liberty and surely a writer and editor whom any supporter of freedom of expression should embrace. Yet Wilkes did not exactly fit the mould set by the pious supporters of ethical, public-interest journalism today. He was also something of a scoundrel — a notorious heavy-drinking rake, gambler, womaniser and debtor, not averse to sorting out differences of opinion by duelling with pistols. The targets of his vitriolic pen were not only royalists, but also the Scots. And the publications that got him into so much trouble with the authorities, and became *causes célèbres* in the struggle for a free press, ranged from scurrilous gossip and half-lies to upper-class pornography.

To borrow the grown up language that has been employed about writers of late, it seems unlikely that anybody would have seen fit to describe Wilkes as one of "the goodies" of journalism or politics. He would certainly never have passed the "but..." test of ethics which many now want to apply before granting the right to press freedom. Let us look briefly at the evidence as to which "breed" of journalist John Wilkes might be considered part of today.

In an age when Members of Parliament were not even paid wages, never mind expenses, Wilkes became the MP for Aylesbury in 1757 after the seat was effectively granted to him by his friend and fellow hell-raiser Thomas Potter—this being the age of "rotten boroughs" when few had the right to vote and elections could be bought and sold. The pair were notorious around the fleshpots of London, Bath and Tunbridge Wells, Potter (an archbishop's son) declaring that Wilkes had "done everything in his power to destroy his health by strong soups, filthy claret, rakish hours, and bad example".[6]

As an MP, Wilkes' positions of public responsibility included that of governor of Aylesbury's foundling hospital—"a suitable position, it was remarked, since he was accountable for so many foundlings".[7] Fathering numerous children out of wedlock was the least of the married MP's vices. Potter had introduced Wilkes to a debauched group of gentlemen reprobates known as the Hellfire Club, who drank, fornicated and indulged in black mass at an old Gothic abbey. Meeting Wilkes years later, the historian Edward Gibbon noted that the older man had hardly mellowed: "A thorough profligate in principle as in practice, his life is stained with every vice and his conversation full of blasphemy and bawdry. These morals he glorifies in, for shame is a weakness he has long surmounted". Lord knows what *Spitting Image* or *Have I Got News For You* would have made of him. Gibbon, however, concluded that "I scarcely ever met a better companion".[8]

The publication that was to write Wilkes' name into the history of press freedom, *The North Briton*, was not launched from entirely pure journalistic motives. Having failed to obtain a government post through patronage, Wilkes turned instead to taking money from one of the government's leading opponents, Lord Temple, for attacking the administration. The government of Lord Bute of the Court Party had launched its own mouthpiece, called *The Briton*. Wilkes used Temple's money to publish *The North Briton*, anonymously, as a lampooning response.

The first issue of *The North Briton* declared that "the liberty of the press" was "the birthright of every Briton". Wilkes himself unashamedly used that birthright to take some liberties with the facts. Adam Smith, the political economist, reported that Wilkes had told him, "Give me a grain of truth and I will mix it up with a great mass of falsehood so that no chemist will ever be able to separate them".[9] That ought to make the authors of today's codes of ethical conduct blanch. We can only wonder at how Lord Justice Leveson and his legal and celebrity camp followers might react if Wilkes had appeared before his Inquiry to boast of mixing a "grain of truth" with "a great mass of falsehood". Some might even sniff that Wilkes was a "different breed" from them. And they would be right, though not in the sense they mean.

In 1762–63 Wilkes' paper won readers and a reputation for its caustic political satire aimed at the government of Lord Bute. The aims of *The North Briton*, the suppression of which was to become key to the battle for press freedom in Britain, had little to do with ethical journalism or the public interest. Rather, in the words of one biographer, Wilkes used his journal "to expose and ridicule the new government's conduct of affairs; to harry the Scots on each and every occasion; to heap all manner of abuse and ridicule on the government and its friends — on Lord Bute in particular, whose alleged intimacy with the King's mother, the Princess Dowager, was a subject of constant comment".[10] It is hard to imagine today's much-maligned tabloids, condemned for their interest in "salacious gossip", running scurrilous stories implying that the prime minister was "romping" with senior members of the royal family.

Wilkes' commitment to publishing what he wanted and his readers enjoyed earned him a trip to the Tower of London in 1763, after issue Number 45 of *The North Briton* carried an account of King George's speech to the opening of parliament. Any printed criticism of the monarch or his government was liable to attract a charge of "seditious libel". Wilkes' anonymous article in No 45, though making clear that its target was the ministers who had written the King's speech rather than the majestic person of George III himself, was interpreted as having called the King a liar. The government issued one of its infamous "general warrants" and almost 50 people suspected of being connected with *The North Briton* were arrested. Identified as the editor of No 45, John Wilkes MP was arrested, his house was ransacked of papers, and he was sent to the Tower. Appearing in court days later, Wilkes declared with typical immodesty that "the liberty of all peers and gentlemen, and, what touches me more sensibly, that of all the middling and inferior set of people, who stand most in need of protection, is in my case this day to be finally decided on a question of such importance as to determine at once whether English Liberty shall be a reality or a shadow".[11] Wilkes' campaign against his treatment would eventually lead to the end of the system of arbitrary politically-motivated arrests under general warrants.

Yet at the same time as he was engaged in this noble struggle over the freedom of the press to report on high politics without state repression, Wilkes was also being condemned and convicted by the House of Lords for printing a "pornographic libel" that went a little further than your average Page 3 photograph.

After his release from the Tower, Wilkes had set up a printing press in his own London house. His plan was to reprint the collected 45 editions of *The North Briton* in one volume, as a fund-raiser. At the same time he instructed the printer to run off a dozen copies of an obscene and blasphemous poem entitled "An Essay on Woman" — a parody of Pope's "Essay on Man" — the authorship of which he fictitiously ascribed to the Bishop of Gloucester. The quality of the verse can perhaps be judged by this excerpt:

> "Let us (since life can little more supply
> Than just a few good fucks, and then we die)
> Expatiate free o'er that loved scene of man
> A mighty maze for mighty pricks to scan"

Only a section of the poem was ever printed, but there were also some additional verses of similar quality, including a bawdy version of "The Universal Prayer" which ended thus:

"To thee, whose fucks throughout all space
This dying world supplies,
One chorus let all beings raise,
All pricks in reverence rise."[12]

Wilkes probably did not write the poetry himself, though it is thought that he did add some notes attacking government politicians of the day in a similar spirit. It seems he only intended to circulate the few copies privately, probably to some of his old drinking-and-fornicating pals from the Hellfire Club. However, in an early example of the perils of mixing up the private and the public, now familiar to many regretful users of Facebook and Twitter, Wilkes forgot that once something is published it is hard to put back in the bottle. A copy inevitably found its way into the hands of his enemies, one of whom, the Earl of Sandwich—himself a reprobate and former Hellfire member—read it aloud in the House of Lords in horrified tones. Their lordships unanimously condemned it as "a most scandalous, obscene and impious libel".

At the same time, the House of Commons resolved that No 45 of Wilkes' *The North Briton* was "a false, scandalous, and seditious libel" and ordered it to be publicly burnt by the Common Hangman at the Royal Exchange. When the officials attempted to carry out these orders, however, a large crowd of Wilkes' supporters from "the middling and inferior set of people" gathered and pelted them with wood and dirt, smashed up the sheriffs' coach and rescued Number 45 from the bonfire. Their affinity for "Wilkes and Liberty" was not, it seemed, dampened by his association with obscene and blasphemous libels. The willingness of the London populace to riot in defence of the scurrilous Wilkes seems a far cry from the sympathetic attitude to a crackdown on tabloid journalists among prominent civil liberties campaigners today.

Meanwhile Wilkes, having been shot in the groin whilst duelling with an angry opponent, escaped to France. He was expelled from parliament, and then declared an outlaw in England. When eventually he returned to London he was jailed for his publishing crimes. While Wilkes continued to enjoy drinking, feasting and entertaining lady visitors from within his prison cell, his supporters outside staged a fortnight of rioting in London, culminating in "the massacre of St George's Fields" in 1768 when troops were ordered to fire into the protesting crowd, killing several people. In response the crowd attacked and pulled down the houses of two Southwark magistrates deemed responsible.

Following his release from prison Wilkes was four times elected as MP for Middlesex. Yet the House of Commons deemed him unfit for office, refused to let him take his seat, and voted instead to hand it to his beaten opponent from the King's Party, parliament taking upon itself the right to ignore not only the disenfranchised masses, but the few freemen who enjoyed the right to vote and had used it to elect Wilkes. This was another historic struggle that the roguish Wilkes was eventually to win over the King and the Court Party, taking his seat in 1774 and forcing parliament to concede forever that it had no right to refuse entry to a legally elected MP.

In the midst of the long battle over his right to represent those who had elected him in parliament, Wilkes found himself — or rather, placed himself — at the centre of the struggle to report the proceedings of parliament to the world outside. It would be hard to exaggerate the importance of this issue for the development of freedom and democracy in Britain. Without the right to publish what is said and done in parliament, how could the people hope to hold their rulers to account? When reporters were finally officially recognised in parliament in 1787, Edmund Burke was reported to have said that "there were Three Estates in Parliament [the Bishops, Lords and MPs]; but, in the Reporters' Gallery yonder, there sat a Fourth Estate more important far than they all".[13]

The public reporting of parliamentary speeches and debates was still officially banned in Wilkes' day, most recently by a parliamentary resolution of 1728. However, as the number of newspapers in London grew, so did their unofficial reports from parliament; during the 1740s Dr Samuel Johnson penned satirical versions of parliamentary proceedings in the *Gentle-*

man's Magazine, thinly disguised under the title "Debates of the Senate of Magna Lilliputia".

In February 1771 Colonel George Onslow, a supporter of the government, demanded in the House of Commons that the resolution of 1728 should be enforced to silence these insolent reporters. Two papers, the *Middlesex Journal* and the *Gazetteer*, not only reported this suggestion but ascribed it to "little cocking George Onslow". How might political figures who complain of being ill-used by the relatively polite press today react to such a cocking little insult?

Outraged MPs demanded that the printers of the two papers concerned and six other newspaper printers should attend parliament to be dealt with for the offence of reporting what was said there. Two printers failed to turn up and apologise, and warrants were issued for their arrest. It was then that Wilkes, now an elected Alderman of the City of London, intervened with a devious scheme to stage-manage a conflict with his old adversaries in parliament that would establish the freedom to report their proceedings. Wilkes and his allies among the City authorities—notably Lord Mayor Brass Crosby and Alderman Richard Oliver—helped to set up the arrest of the printers, and then made a great show of refusing to hand them over to the parliamentary authorities, insisting that the summons and arrests were illegal within the City of London. In response Lord Mayor Colby and Alderman Oliver were summoned to Westminster—though Wilkes was the main mover in this affair, the parliamentary authorities did not want that troublemaker anywhere near the place. The City men went to Westminster attended by huge crowds of supporters.

Parliament first sent Alderman Oliver to the Tower, after he refused to respond to the charges, saying "You may do as you please. I defy you". Then Lord Mayor Crosby, whose hearing had been delayed by a severe bout of gout, went back to Westminster to learn his fate. There were unheard-of riotous scenes outside parliament as he arrived, with government ministers and MPs attacked and their carriages smashed. The *Middlesex Journal* reported that a crowd of 50,000 laid siege to parliament to defend the liberties at stake with more than polite words, even coming close to lynching Lord North, the prime minister: "Lord North's chariot glasses were broken to pieces, as was the carriage soon afterwards, by which he received a wound, and was exceedingly terrified. The populace also took off his hat and cut it into pieces, and he narrowly escaped with his life".[14] Whilst thousands of Londoners besieged parliament and violently assaulted the prime minister in defence of press freedom, there is no record of anybody having attacked a newspaper publisher with a shaving-foam "pie" at that time, which is apparently what passes for radical protest on these issues around Westminster today.

Amid these riotous scenes, parliament voted to send the Lord Mayor to join Alderman Oliver in the Tower of London, condemned as if they were traitors for refusing to cooperate with state repression of the press. While they were held in the Tower there were public demonstrations in their support, and effigies of the Princess Dowager, the Speaker of the Commons, the Attorney general and assorted leading lords and MPs were beheaded by a chimney-sweep dressed as a cleric on Tower Hill, then burnt. When the two City Aldermen were released after six weeks, they emerged to a 21-gun salute and much public celebration. Despite "winning" the case, the Westminster authorities had been humbled. The defiant printers had gone unpunished. And the newspapers carried on printing reports from parliament. Wilkes' campaign had won an historic victory for the right of the press and the people to hold their rulers to account.

John Wilkes, then, was a pornographer, a rake, an all-round scoundrel and a political opportunist, perfectly willing to defame and to fudge the truth in his writing in order to settle scores or advance his cause, often pursuing selfish motives and petty quarrels wrapped up in the public language of defending great liberties and a free press. There is little doubt that he misused that freedom and, to cite Lord Justice Leveson's words, "abused those vital rights", by exploiting the free press for his own less-than-noble purposes.

Yet Wilkes and his ignoble publications helped to change the course of political history and struck a mighty blow for press freedom. In this he was backed by large sections of a public who, far from standing by or applauding as the legal and political authorities went after journalists and the popular press, repeatedly rioted to prevent the rascal Wilkes and his allies being denied their liberties.

The likes of Wilkes offended everything that was dear to the courtly elite of their day. They would hardly have lived up to the high ethical standards we hear being demanded of journalists today, either. In some ways he was rather closer to that "other breed" of reporters that are now described as rats and scum and peddlers of filth. If anything his stand for the freedom of the press reminds me more of that taken by Larry Flynt, the American pornographer and publisher of *Hustler* magazine. Flynt has fought many legal cases to defend his publications against censorship on free speech grounds, arguing that "If the First Amendment [to the US Constitution, which enshrines freedom of speech and the press] will protect a scumbag like me, it will protect all of you". Wilkes was to be a great inspiration to the American revolutionaries who wrote that Amendment, though no such civilised attitude to freedom of expression ever made it into UK law.

For my money John Wilkes, the scoundrel and publisher of filth, who enjoyed mixing an ounce of truth with "a great mass of falsehood", was more of a moral force for good than any attempt to limit the freedom of the press in the name of ethics, or any high-handed attempts to force it to conform to somebody else's standards. His is a tale of making the best of the messy pursuit of freedom in the real world. Wilkes' story is also a reminder that it has always been kings and courtiers, or their modern elitist equivalents, who are keenest to impose restraints on what a free press can tell the public, generally in the name of decency or moral probity. There are "cocking little Onslows" abroad today too, all of whom profess to believe in press freedom, "but…"

Freedom of Expression? "Absurd!"

Many people have been appalled by the revelations of press malpractice around the phone-hacking scandal. More concerning to me, however, has been how few now seem prepared to mount a resolute defence of the freedom of the press in response to the furore.

The Leveson Inquiry has been widely presented as a neutral forum for public investigation of the "culture and ethics" of the UK media. Some even tried to portray it as a radical body representing the public against the press barons. In fact the Leveson hearings were an act of powerful state interference in the affairs of the British press. The Inquiry, as will be argued in a later chapter, has been more like an inquisition designed to root out heretics and impose a conformist orthodoxy on the press, akin to a show trial in which the tabloid sinners were found guilty before the first witness was called.

Anybody with a passing knowledge of the history of the struggle for press freedom from state control should immediately have recognised the Leveson Inquiry, not as an "opportunity" or a potential ally of progressive reform, but as the enemy of a free press. Lord Justice Leveson and his army of lawyers and political and celebrity backers might insist they support freedom of expression. Yet in seeking to limit how that freedom might be exercised, they stand in the same tradition as those who tried to control the press in the past by banning, licensing, taxing or otherwise restraining newspapers.

Why, then, were there so few voices raised against this inquisition masquerading as an inquiry? Instead the "I believe in press freedom, but…" lobby, with its battle-cry "For our Lord Justice Leveson, St Hugh, and the public interest!" seemed to have swept the field and cowed the opposition. We looked in vain for the modern incarnations of the heroes who risked all to fight for a free press in centuries past. There was little sign of a John Milton, John Wilkes, Tom Paine or J.S. Mill for today, who could take up the cudgels against attempts to wash the press's mouth out with soap.

Relatively few such heroes have been evident in our quality media, where many allegedly liberal voices went over to the side of Lord Justice Leveson and the state in this battle. Journalists and broadcasters who might normally enjoy sneering at celebrity culture apparently converted to become excitable groupies for celebrities bashing the tabloids. A media which has often appeared keen to nail the police for trampling on liberties seemed overnight to become cheerleaders for Metropolitan Police action against tabloid journalists and newspapers.

Nor are there many uncompromising champions of a free press to be found among our prominent civil liberties lobbyists today. Many campaigners appeared keen to sign up as Lord Justice Leveson's camp followers. The leading lady of UK civic society, Shami Chakrabarti of the lobby group Liberty, looked less like a fighter for freedom than a member of the Crown's Star Chamber as she sat alongside a former police chief and media grandees on the Leveson Inquiry panel appointed to sit in judgement on the tabloid press. Elsewhere there seemed a symbolic irony in watching a video of Hugh Grant doing his tabloid-bashing act at the Lib Dem conference, demanding the "scumbags" of the popular press be driven into "the North Sea", in front of a banner emblazoned with the name of the campaign Index on Censorship.

Resolute defenders of press freedom are certainly not much in evidence among the ranks of journalism academics. Seemingly blinded by their own anti-tabloid bigotry and Murdoch-phobia, many from the avowedly liberal quarters of higher education have sat on their hands—or worse, used them to applaud Leveson's show trial of popular journalism.

With some honourable exceptions, professors and lecturers in journalism and journalism studies at UK universities and colleges have emerged as leading players in the push for more regulation of the press. That these public guardians of journalism's future, entrusted with inculcating new generations with sound principles and opening young minds, should have effectively deserted the cause of press freedom seems more depressing to me than what an unprincipled private investigator gets up to. Little wonder that Mr Mosley generously conceded he would be happy to have journalism academics on his proposed powerful new statutory-backed press regulation authority.

One of the most disquieting things that I have heard said around the phone-hacking scandal did not come from a tabloid journalist, or a victim of press excesses. It came from the Director of Journalism at the Reuters Institute for the Study of Journalism at the University of Oxford.

John Lloyd (for it is he) is no old-fashioned conservative bigot. He is a lettered man of the Left, a former Communist who was editor of the *New Statesman* and became the *Financial Times'* social conscience before ascending the Ivory Towers at Oxford. Wearing his Reuters Director of Journalism hat, Lloyd wrote the preface for a collection of responses to the phone-hacking scandal published early in 2012, a short piece headed, in mock-tabloid style, "Exposed: The 'Swaggering Arrogance' of the Popular Press". Here Lloyd let rip at the culture and ethics of the press, and expressed the hope that Leveson, the courts and "public pressure for a better journalism for all" could yet save the day.

In the middle of this, Lloyd lambasted the supposed presumption among journalists that "whatever they were prevented from doing was an expression of censorship or worse". Fair enough perhaps; there has been no shortage of self-importance and self-righteousness across the press, as we will discuss later. But then Lloyd declared that this arrogant attitude "was best expressed by a sentence in the Press Complaints Commission code, which stated flatly that 'freedom of expression is itself a public good' – an absurd claim, but brilliantly expressive of the working philosophy of many newspapers".[15]

A leading journalist turned top journalism academic flatly states – with what some might even consider "swaggering arrogance" – that the notion that "freedom of expression is itself a public good" is frankly "absurd". Perhaps that captures the depth of the problem, the swelling scale of the "Buts" summed up in one sentence, if not in one word. The principle that there is something inherently good about a free press is "absurd". The belief that freedom of expression is an inalienable, indivisible right on which all of our public liberties rest is "absurd". If only John Wilkes and the rest of the unruly fighters for a free press could have appreciated the Director of Journalism's words of wisdom in centuries past, it might have saved them all a lot of trouble. After all, why bother going to the Tower to defend an absurdity?

The PCC Code's clear statement of support for freedom of expression as a public good was arguably the single point in the document that mattered and the one that should be defended above all others. Instead it has been singled out as the point to denounce. Lloyd's dismissal of it as "absurd" might be a startling revelation of how far things have gone down the slippery slope in journalism academia, but he is hardly alone on that journey. Other journalism academics argue that the press should be, if not actually licensed, at least regulated in the same way as the legal profession—which could presumably involve restricting journalism to those with special qualifications, "striking off" those who failed to meet the standards set by the authorities, and all the other rules and restrictions involved in regulating a "closed" profession. Farewell to the idea of journalism as simply the formal extension of freedom of expression, which ought to be open to anybody with a brain and a laptop, and welcome to the world of journalism as a professional guild, closed to all but those who pass the ethical tests set by the professors. As if the domination of the mainstream media by the privately educated middle classes wasn't problem enough, it seems we may now have to cope with a different type of "closed shop" as well.

What seems truly absurd is for those who devote their time and energy to lobbying for tougher codes, rules, regulators, laws, ombudsmen or licences for the press to still insist on beginning every statement with "Of course I believe in a free press, but…" It might be better if they were to follow their own strictures about the fundamental need for honesty, come clean and say that, actually, they don't. Once we all know where we stand, the battle over press freedom can commence in earnest.

Tolerance — And Telling it Like it is

None of this is intended to deny that there are serious short-comings in the UK press. Some of us have spent countless thousands of words exposing them and berating the media for its prejudices and poisons over the years. But the far bigger issue in the atmosphere of today is freedom of expression. Defending a free press does not mean endorsing what it does. You are not obliged to buy, read, look up or like any of it. Better to have a free press you are free to hate, however, than a conformist one you could not care less about.

Leave aside for the moment such extraordinary events as the hacking of the murdered teenager Milly Dowler's phone and other offences that can be left to PC Plod. In principle, what is the problem with the press? Many are infuriated by the fashion for intrusive reporting and exhibitionist interviews, the obsession with elevating celebrity trivia and exposing the love lives and cellulite of the (wannabe) rich and famous (for being famous). Yet for others, this sort of entertainment-news is what they enjoy. They in turn might object to the more acerbic columnists or cartoonists who ridicule and upset people for a living. Those same professional controversialists, however, might be the main attraction for some.

The point of living with a free press is that you don't need to insist on any particular version of it, or to impose your views of what the press ought to be on to other people. It is nobody's business to police the views and preferences of others by, for example, seeking to reform or close down the newspapers that suit the tastes of millions. A pluralist media of mixed tastes and opinions that might occasionally upset your indigestion will always be healthier than a sterile conformist one that can give you a stiff neck from permanently gazing up at it striking poses on the moral high ground.

Many of those who campaign against the tabloid press today also talk about the need for greater "diversity" in the media. Their focus is on the centralised ownership of the press by giant media corporations. Monopoly control of the market is certainly a big problem. But what is missing most in the media is diversity of content and opinion. Regardless of ownership, there is too often a sterile atmosphere of conformity bordering on uniformity over the serious media, something which can look like what Orwell called "a general tacit agreement that 'it wouldn't do' to mention that particular fact" or opinion.

Much of the "free press, but…" lobby is really expressing its own intolerance in the phoney language of liberalism. In response, let us encourage instead an open-minded attitude of genuine tolerance towards the media and society. But to be tolerant of different opinions and attitudes is not the same thing as passively putting up with whatever they say. It is possible to be uncompromisingly for a free press and the right to be offensive, and at the same time to exercise your freedom of expression to lay into the media.

In short there should be no contradiction between tolerating the views of others, and telling it like it is with no holds barred from your point of view.

In today's hyper-sensitive, thin-skinned culture you are more likely to hear the argument that, yes, we should support free speech, "but" that does not mean you are free to condemn or offend others. In the run-up to the 2010 General Election the New Labour government issued a consultation paper on "People and Power". This document recognised "freedom of expression" as an important British value. However, it insisted, that freedom comes with responsibilities — to "be non-judgemental, open and encouraging", to avoid "forcing our opinions on others" and to "accept the consequences of being outspoken". In other words, freedom of expression is dependent on not being too outspoken, critical or intemperate, and if you do offend others, you must accept the punitive consequences.[16]

Yet freedom of expression does not entail any such responsibility to be "non-judgemental" or inoffensive. And defending those freedoms does not mean you have to endorse what is published, or that you cannot hammer what the media or anybody might say and do from here to Denmark and back.

I mention Denmark because of the instructive controversy over the Danish cartoons which caused an international storm in 2005. The *Jyllands-Posten* newspaper first published 12 controversial cartoons about Islam, most of them depicting the prophet Mohammed. It claimed they were intended to contribute to the discussion of media self-censorship of anything that might offend Muslims. The cartoons were subsequently reproduced elsewhere. They sparked a worldwide controversy resulting in protests, violence, diplomatic incidents and trade boycotts, especially after Danish Imams toured the Middle East highlighting the "outrage".

The Danish cartoons also gave rise to a falsely polarised debate about freedom of expression. On one hand there were those who said that these cartoons were deliberately offensive and that the papers had no right to publish them. On the other were those who claimed that, on the contrary, publishing these cartoons was the essence of what a free press should be about. Both were wrong.

The Danish newspapers were entirely entitled to publish the Mohammed cartoons, and we should defend their right to do so and reject any notion of censorship or punishment. But we should also feel free to tell them that it was a pointless, counter-productive thing to do, more like a tantrum of protest than a considered political statement. They were not, despite the newspaper's claim, a contribution to any discussion.

I have written in defence of the right to be offensive to Islam and anything else since the Salman Rushdie *Satanic Verses* controversy broke more than 20 years ago. These cartoons, however, were inviting offence for its own sake. They were an infantile gesture designed to stick a finger up to Islam, courting theatrically outraged reactions without making any worthwhile point. It was a "brave" stand for freedom of the press in the same way that putting a picture of a tumescent Pope wearing a condom on the front page would be, and a contribution to the discussion about the West and Islam on an intellectual par with urinating on a copy of the Koran. There are surely better ways to cause offence and get a reaction than that. (Unlike comedians who go out of their way to offend, the papers could not even offer the defence that the cartoons were only a joke.)

In short the Danish press had the right to publish those cartoons—yet in the circumstances they were arguably wrong to exercise that right, and the UK press was justified (for once) in refusing to publish them afterwards. That is the proper spirit of combined tolerance and judgementalism required in a free press.

Freedom is always a messy business, filled with close judgement calls, contradictions and the need to defend it for things you don't like. But the bottom line is that infringements on that freedom are always worse and more dangerous to our society than the most egregious abuse of freedom might be. If there is one thing worse than a free press, it is the alternative. It is time to make the moral case for more press freedom, not less.

The truth is that, whatever your preferred tastes in the press might be, by far the biggest problem with the British press is that it is not nearly free or open enough. Contrary to the impression often given today, the UK media in all of its forms is not too free to run wild and invade people's privacy, or too much at liberty to say and do whatever it feels like, or too ready to let offensive opinions run riot. It does not need tighter regulation, or new laws.

There are already far too many formal and informal constraints on a free press, from England's execrable libel laws—the envy of autocrats the world over—to the culture of You Can't Say That which pervades the political and media class. And even more importantly, there is already a far too closed and conformist atmosphere hanging over the media, which threatens to become thicker and more incapacitating still as an outcome of the Leveson Inquiry. Whether some want to hear it or not, we need more press freedom for all, not less.

How far things have gone in consolidating the "press freedom, but…" atmosphere we live under became clear in February 2012 when reporter Nick Davies was announced as the winner of the Paul Foot Award for investigative journalism, for his central role in exposing the phone-hacking scandal.

According to a glowing report of his triumph, "The organising committee, in its citation, praised Davies' 'dogged and lonely reporting', the impact of which forced 'a humbled Rupert Murdoch' to close the *News of the World…*".[17] When a serious journalist wins a top investigative award partly for helping to close down Britain's best-selling newspaper, we are a long way from the prize of a free press with no "buts".

1   Lord Justice Leveson's opening statement on the first day of the Inquiry's hearings, 14 November 2011 (http://www.levesoninquiry. org.uk/wp-content/uploads/2011/11/Transcript-of-Morning-Hearing-14-November-2011.txt).

2   George Orwell, *The Freedom of the Press*, 1945 (http://orwell.ru/ library/novels/Animal_Farm/english/efp_go).

3   James S. Ettema and Theodore L. Glasser, *Custodians of Conscience: Investigative Journalism and Public Virtue*, Columbia University Press 1998.

4   *The Times*, 27 February 2012.

5   See *The Week*, 1 December 2011 (http://www.theweek.co.uk/ media/leveson-inquiry/43174/shock-horror-tabloid-hacks-are-new-paedophiles); Kevin Marsh, 'Getting the thugs off the street' in Richard Lance Keeble and John Mair (eds.) *The Phone-Hacking Scandal: Journalism on Trial*, arima publishing 2012, p. 83.

6   Quoted in Louis Kronenberger, *The Extraordinary Mr Wilkes*, New English Library 1974, p. 7.

7   *Ibid.*, p. 11.

8   *Ibid.*, p. 28.

9   *Ibid.*, p. 33.

10   George Rude, *Wilkes and Liberty*, Lawrence and Wishart 1983 edition, p. 21.

11   *Ibid.*, p. 27.

12   Cited in *The Extraordinary Mr Wilkes*, pp. 54–55.

13   Cited in Thomas Carlyle, *On Heroes, Hero-Worship, & the Heroic in History*, 1840, Dent 1908 edition, p. 392.

14   Cited in *Wilkes and Liberty*, p. 162.

15   *The Phone-Hacking Scandal: Journalism on Trial*, p. 3.

16   *People and Power: Shaping Democracy, Rights and Responsibilities*, Ministry of Justice, March 2010.

17   The *Guardian*, 28 February 2012.

Chapter Two

Whose Ethics Are They Anyway?

When Richard Desmond, well-known purveyor of "adult" entertainments and proprietor of the *Express* and the *Star* newspapers and Channel 5 television, appeared at the Leveson Inquiry, he was asked about ethical journalism. "Well, ethical, I don't quite know what the word means," said Desmond, "but perhaps you'll explain what the word means, ethical." The spectacle of a porn merchant confessing that he was confused as to the meaning of ethics inevitably caused much amusement.[1]

On closer inspection, however, it turns out that Desmond the press-and-porn baron had a point. It is no simple matter clearly to define what we mean by "ethical" in any sphere of life, and perhaps in journalism more than most.

The "press freedom, but..." lobby sermonise about the virtues of "ethical journalism" pursued in "the public interest". The implication is that the full benefits of press freedom should be enjoyed only by those who meet these criteria. Many of them want to see the authorities enforce more rigorous rules and ethical codes for good journalism. Some want to see the meaning of the public interest defined in law, both to protect "ethical public-interest journalism" and to punish those publications that misuse the term as a cover for their scurrilous activities.

Ethical journalism sounds a powerful and attractive concept. Who, after all, could be in favour of something called "unethical" journalism? Everybody wants to present their work as ethical journalism in the public interest; Rupert Murdoch

accused the *Daily Mail* of being "unethical" in his evidence to
Leveson. Ethics must be a good thing, right? Maybe, but these
things are rarely as straightforward as they are presented.

An unspoken truth of the debate about press regulation is
that talk of "ethics" is generally a charade, a snow-job. Ethics is
being used as a whiter-than-white banner behind which campaigners for media reform and regulation can conceal their own
agendas. Their fetishised notion of ethics enables them to
express their particular political and sectional interests in the
idealised language of universal values.

The demand for "ethical journalism" is essentially a cultural
manifesto masquerading as morality. In dressing up their
particular interests in the garb of "the public interest", ethics
man and woman are rather like the doctors who used to wear
the white coats of their healing profession while advertising the
health benefits of smoking a particular brand of cigarettes.

The ethical crusaders often attack tabloid reporters for the
practice of "blagging" — pretending to be somebody else in
order to get what they want. Yet in putting on the cloak of ethics
and posing as high-minded figures with only the public interest
at heart, they are doing some questionable blagging of their
own. They are using inoffensive, bland-sounding notions of
ethical journalism to smuggle in some reprehensible ideas about
purging the press.

The argument in this chapter is that, although some would
have us believe otherwise, nobody in this debate has a disinterested or neutral view of the media and press freedom. There has
been a long list of official investigations into the press in Britain
since the Second World War, from the first Royal Commission
on the Press (1947–49) to the Leveson Inquiry of 2011–12. Every
one of them has claimed to conduct a dispassionate inquiry into
the standards and workings of the press, representing the
general public interest. Yet in reality every inquiry has been
shaped by the particular cultural climate of the moment when it
took place and driven by the prevailing political winds of the
day. If the first Royal Commission of the late 1940s was
essentially a Labour Party operation aimed at nobbling the Tory

press barons, the second one in the early 1960s was largely a Tory stunt launched to undermine trade union influence in the print industry. Why should we believe that the Leveson Inquiry is a "neutral" exception to that historical rule of political motives?

Talk of imposing tighter ethical codes on the media has itself become a polite code for expressing an agenda of purging the press—an agenda which somebody lacks the courage or the conviction to propose in its own name. They have got away with this masquerade for too long because too few have been prepared to point out that the ethical emperor has no clothes.

Religious fundamentalists often claim that their disgust at homosexuality or abortion stems from these things going "against the word of God". Thus they project their personal prejudices and preferences onto a higher source of authority. Though the prejudices they express might be quite different, those attacking the popular press for offending against "ethical journalism" seem to be doing much the same thing. They are projecting their personal tastes and sensibilities on to the secular god of "ethics".

Judgement Calls

Is it possible to have a simple definition of what is ethical journalism or what we mean by the public interest that can be made into general rules for the conduct of the press? The simple answer is: probably not, no.

We might just about all agree on an ethical bottom line. For example, that it is unethical to hack into the phone messages of a teenage girl who has been abducted and is feared dead. But that seems a pretty low moral base. Those who commissioned or carried out the hacking of Milly Dowler's phone have not sought to defend it on ethical or any other grounds. The single person on the planet who has publicly defended it is the former *News of the World* journalist Paul McMullan. So the moral divide on that issue appears to be the Whole World versus one reviled hack. Not much of a basis for an all-encompassing ethical code, is it?

Go beyond that baseline in trying to detail an ethical code for the press, however, and things get slightly more complicated. Of course all organisations and institutions have developed standards and rules. The press is no exception. Except that with journalism, existing codes of practice tend to be fairly careful in their prescriptions — for good reasons.

In the real world of the media, questions about the right reporting method to employ or the right story to publish do not fit neatly into tick-boxes. What is the best way to use press freedom is something best judged by journalists and their audience in response to the questions of the day. It is often not an issue that can be decided in advance according to a predetermined checklist.

Many questions of how to behave in the circumstances cannot easily be answered by reference to a code of pure press ethics apparently drafted on a cloud, floating far above the grubby streets below.

For example, everybody agrees that phone-hacking is evil and that using private detectives to dig dirt is inexcusable. Or perhaps not. We now know that not only the lowly tabloid *News of the World* used phone-hacking methods to pursue stories when it chose to. Even a top reporter at the high-minded *Guardian* has admitted to doing the same and hacking a target's phone messages, in pursuit of what he saw as the public interest — "for ethical reasons, not tittle-tattle".[2] Apparently evil can become ethical in the right circumstances.

It has also been admitted that News Corp was not the only large media institution to employ dubious private detectives to help in its investigations. No less an august body than the BBC has admitted doing the same thing on 230 occasions, in pursuit of what its Director-General described as "the public interest", of course.[3] The inexcusable can apparently be excused by evoking the public interest.

It is important to have principles, and we all hope that our work is guided by our own. In practice those principles have to exist alongside the recognition that there is no substitute for judgement calls. The question of whether splashing a sensational story or using a questionable reporting tactic is justified can only be decided in the particular context where the question arises.

Those grappling with the problem of how to impose black-and-white rules about what journalists can and cannot do are playing with fire. In a major lecture on the future of the press, the ethics expert Professor Onora O'Neill has proposed that the law should be able to regulate, not the content of the press, but the process and methods it uses to obtain its stories, effectively outlawing a list of investigative practices.[4] The Leveson Inquiry made clear that it would scrutinise not only phone-hacking but also other illegal and "unethical" reporting methods, including subterfuge, "blagging" and the payment of witnesses.

The truth is, however, that any ethical code or law which sought to rule out in advance such underhand and questionable methods would almost certainly have made it impossible to pursue and publish some of the most famous news stories and scandals of the past two centuries.

Take, for example, the Victorian newspaper exposé which helped press the UK parliament to pass a law raising the age of consent to 16 and introducing new measures against child prostitution. In 1885 W.T. Stead, the sensationalist editor of the *Pall Mall Gazette*, launched an investigation into child prostitution in London with the support of the Social Purity Movement. He published a dramatic series of articles, entitled "The Maiden Tribute of Modern Babylon", which caused a national scandal and drove parliament to action. WH Smith refused to have the "obscene" paper on its news-stands, though Salvation Army members and other volunteers helped to sell out the issues.

The *Pall Mall Gazette*'s style was a mixture of puffed-up moralism with puerile titillation, of eager voyeurism presented as horrified disgust, of a type we have become familiar with in the modern media. The articles were advertised thus: "All those who are squeamish, and all those who are prudish, and all those who would prefer to live in a fool's paradise of imaginary innocence and purity, selfishly oblivious to the horrible realities which torment those whose lives are passed in the London inferno, will do well not to read the *Pall Mall Gazette* of Monday and the three following days." They were published under such salacious headings as "The Violation of Virgins", "Confessions of a Brothel-keeper", and, most shockingly, "A Girl of 13 Bought for £5". To obtain that last story, Stead employed somewhat unconventional and entirely illegal journalistic methods. He posed as a "procurer" and arranged personally to buy a 13-year-old virgin called Eliza Armstrong for £5 from her alcoholic mother, with the apparent intention to ship the girl to the Continent where she was to be exploited as a prostitute. (Victorian social reformers seemed convinced that, while British girls might be abducted, child prostitution was something which only really went on among filthy foreigners abroad.)[5]

Amid the political uproar that followed, Stead and his accomplices were charged with abduction and procurement—a case prosecuted by the Attorney General himself—and he was sentenced to three months in jail. Although he is now lauded by liberal commentators as a pioneering hero of investigative journalism—one now claims that those who have investigated the heinous crime of phone-hacking have "followed in Stead's footsteps"—it seems unlikely that Stead himself or his methods would have measured up too well to the standards of "ethical journalism" that many now want written in stone if not law. As well as being a Victorian moral crusader of a sort that does not go down well in media circles—a "Puritan chock-full of guile" in the words of one contemporary socialist—Stead's style of journalism was often accused of being sensationalist, prurient and even obscene; or, as some might say these days, "tabloid". His investigation into child prostitution involved cutting corners, breaking laws and fudging facts in a way that might not pass the purity tests of today's media moralists. He was also, like some other famous Victorians, a crank who believed in ghosts and the occult and published spiritualist newspapers which saw him ridiculed as a madman in the years before his fittingly dramatic death aboard the Titanic in 1912. Yet in the circumstances of the time his decision to flout the law and standards of respectable society won widespread support.

There are many other tales of famous investigations whose methods might fall foul of the rules and conventions now being insisted upon by influential voices. Take the Thalidomide scandal, concerning a drug given to pregnant women that caused serious deformities in some children (it had been tested on animals, but not pregnant animals). In the early 1970s, the *Sunday Times* fought a long journalistic and legal battle to expose the full truth and demand justice for the thalidomide children. A decisive factor was the large sum of money that the paper's editor, Harold Evans, paid an informant for confidential documentary dirt on the drug company, Distillers. Even at the time such deals were sneered at as "chequebook journalism", and the struggle to publish the leaked information went to the highest courts in the UK and Europe. Today, as *Times* journalist Camilla Cavendish has observed, "Sir Harry would have to be extra brave to pay his whistleblower £8,000 to get files from Distillers", since "the Bribery Act 2010 makes it illegal to pay for information that could reveal corruption. Had it come into force two years earlier, it would have prevented *The Daily Telegraph* from paying for the information that exposed the MPs' expenses scandal".[6] That Act was passed into law even before the furore about the evils of newspapers bribing officials and paying for stories began. What price the Thalidomide exposé today?

Every big story from Watergate to Squidgygate, and just about every other scandal lumbered with the "gate" suffix, generally involves some level of underhand antics by the reporter. After all, these investigative journalists are trying to reveal information that somebody, somewhere (often somewhere high up) wants to keep secret. Before getting too high on Lord Justice Leveson's horse about the offences of "unethical" reporting, it is worth recalling the words of William Randolph Hearst, the Rupert Murdoch of late nineteenth- and early twentieth-century America, a legendary press baron who was the model for Orson Welles' Citizen Kane. "News", declared Hearst, "is something somebody doesn't want printed; all else is advertising".[7] That is a distinction which might seem even more important to bear in mind today, when so much of the celebrity-soaked, PR-driven media looks like advertising in disguise.

The pressurised search to unearth news that "somebody doesn't want printed", and to do so yesterday, can lead editors and journalists to make errors and unwise judgement calls. That does not alter the fact that there will always be circumstances where the story justifies unconventional reporting measures and pushing the "ethical" envelope.

Tabloids, quality newspapers and broadcasters can all get carried away in the zealous pursuit of a story that suits their own agenda. Such mistakes and misjudgements ought to be exposed, but not offered as evidence that future reporting should be more regimented or restrained on ethical grounds. After all, it could happen to anybody. The *News of the World* obviously overstepped every mark in the book with the tactics it used to pursue some stories, most infamously by hacking crime victims' phone messages. But what about the methods certain other publications and broadcasters employed in pursuing the phone-hacking story itself?

By the start of 2012, for example, the *Guardian* had published no fewer than 40 corrections, retractions and apologies in relation to stories it had run about the Murdoch press and the phone-hacking scandal. So over-eager was that noble paper to pursue its campaign that it seemed as willing as celebrity gossip-mongers to rush into print and online with unsubstantiated allegations, rumour and, as they might have it, "tittle-tattle".

The corrections the *Guardian* had to publish included: the withdrawal of the false claim that Murdoch papers had hacked the medical records of former prime minister Gordon Brown's family; an apology for its false front-page claim that the Murdoch-owned *Sun* had stalked a female lawyer from the Leveson Inquiry (which non-existent offence the excited writer had likened to the tabloid "casually defecating on his lordship's desk while doing a thumbs-up sign"[8]); and the withdrawal of a report, published in language no tabloid would use without the obligatory asterisks, which falsely claimed that, before the singer Charlotte Church's sixteenth birthday, the *Sun* "began a public countdown to the day on which she could be legally fucked". (That unsubstantiated story was based on evidence that Church herself gave at the Leveson Inquiry which, as with much of the celebrity gossip offered there, the lawyers and writers present seemed to accept as good coin without checking their facts.)

The most dramatic mistake was the *Guardian*'s claims that the *News of the World* had not only hacked the missing Milly Dowler's phone in 2001 but had deleted key messages from her voicemail, which gave the Dowler family false hope that she was alive. It was these dramatic revelations that led directly to Rupert Murdoch closing down the *News of the World* and David Cameron setting up the Leveson Inquiry. A few months later it became known that the story was not all that it seemed; there was no evidence that the paper had deleted those messages. Nobody, however, suggested that the Inquiry should be closed down and the *NotW* reopened. As my colleague Brendan O'Neill pointed out when exposing these trends, the liberal media appeared to be "using tabloid tactics to slay the tabloids", so that "Leveson and its cheerleaders are starting to look about as reliable as the *Sunday Sport*".[9]

So much for "ethical, public-interest journalism". If they applied the strict journalistic codes they advocate, it seems that some of the media reformers might have to have themselves struck off.

Ethical Smokescreens

The argument that press freedom should effectively be reserved for those who meet defined ethical standards hides behind the notion that ethics are somehow a neutral set of universal values, existing above the everyday fray. But in the real world nobody is entirely neutral. And what are presented as ethics do not come out of the ether. Down here on Earth, ethics are often a shield behind which people scramble for their particular interests.

Ethical questions raised about such matters as privacy, good taste or the public interest are politically contingent. In other words, they mean different things depending on who is raising them and in what circumstances. Concerns expressed about the media and press standards are rarely if ever as disinterested or high-minded as they might appear. These questions are posed less to express timeless values than in response to particular political pressures of the moment.

Whatever lofty principle the restraint and regulation of a free press is supposed to advance at any given moment in history—whether it is to protect God from blasphemy, the King from sedition, the innocent from persecution, the public from sleaze or simply the truth from corruption—we can be fairly sure there is always a rather more earthbound agenda or interest at work behind the most elevated-sounding proposition.

It would be a mistake to take anybody's "ethical" stance on press regulation at face value. When something like the current crisis of the UK press breaks, everybody will jump in with their own ideas and demands about what needs to be done. That is fine. All are entitled to their opinions and it is incumbent on a system of freedom of expression even to allow others to argue for less of it. At the same time, however, the rest of us need to be clear that those arguments are shaped less by universal values than by particular views of the media and the public, reflecting whose side those expressing them happen to be on.

Does anybody seriously believe, for example, that certain politicians and media outlets would have pursued the phone-hacking scandal with such vigour if the Murdoch papers had still been wholeheartedly for Gordon Brown and New Labour at the last general election?

It might seem that the problems of regulating the intrusive press have been a constant feature of British public debate since the Second World War. Three royal commissions and several high-powered committees looked into the press long before the Leveson Inquiry, all on the surface raising similar concerns. A closer look reveals different motives at work at different times. It has always depended upon the political atmosphere in which the debate about the press took place, and which players were behind the inquiring.

Each official investigation into the UK press over the past 65 years has been a politically-driven exercise masquerading as a neutral, objective assessment. All that has changed over time is the nature of the politics doing the driving on different occasions.

Take the first Royal Commission on the press, which ran from 1947 to 1949 and led to the creation of the first General Council of the Press (later called the Press Council, later still replaced by the Press Complaints Commission, now to be replaced by some other body that may have Press in the title). This Royal Commission was set up after the Second World War by the newly-empowered Labour Party and political Left in an effort to tame the Tory press barons. While the issue of press standards was, as usual, put in the foreground of concerns, the underlying aim was to attack the increasing monopolisation of newspaper ownership by big media corporations.

A royal commission was proposed by the National Union of Journalists in 1946, concerned that the growth of "commercial newspapers with millions of circulation has reduced news to the quality of entertainment". The idea of regulating the press was taken up by the first-ever majority Labour government in the atmosphere of general enthusiasm for state-backed planning following the Second World War. Even such a free-market publication as *The Economist* had predicted a post-war regime in which official agencies would give the press "professional guidance... to maintain high standards in the face of propriet-orial pressures, financial considerations, and the contemporary mistranslation of popularity to mean vulgarity". The Left and Right wings of post-war journalism seemed fairly united in both their support for greater state planning and their snobbish con-tempt for the vulgar readership.

The Labour government endorsed the idea of a Royal Commission largely because it was bitter about the role of the press in the 1945 General Election. Tory papers such as the *Daily Mail* and the *Daily Express* had attacked Clement Attlee's

Labour Party throughout the campaign, confidently predicting victory for Winston Churchill's Conservatives right up to the moment when Labour won its first-ever majority in a landslide. The statistics bandied about were that, whereas Labour had won 48 per cent of the votes cast to the Conservatives' 40 per cent, Tory papers accounted for 52 per cent of the market compared to 35 per cent for Labour papers. Hence the Commission was charged by the Labour government with inquiring into and making recommendations on "the control, management and ownership of the newspaper and periodical press and the news agencies, including the financial structure and the monopolistic tendencies in control".[10]

The Labour government's primary agenda in launching that first inquiry, then, was to counter the Tory press barons' "monopolistic tendencies in control" of the press. Would there have been any such Royal Commission if Socialist millionaires had monopolised the press in 1945, and more papers had emulated the Labour-supporting *Daily Mirror*?

The second Royal Commission into the Press was launched in very different circumstances, in 1961, after the Conservatives had been back in power for a decade. Again, concerns about press standards and intrusion were to the fore in the public justification. Once more, however, the authorities had an underlying agenda of their own. Where the Labour government of the late 1940s had sought to use a royal commission to tame the Tory press barons, the Conservative government of the early 1960s was more interested in using it to tame trade union power in the print industry.

The Tory government of Harold McMillan reluctantly bowed to pressure for a second Royal Commission on the press after several newspapers had closed in 1960–61. In a cabinet discussion of February 1961, prime minister MacMillan himself worried that "if the Government were to institute an enquiry… they might appear to be giving way to pressure and they would run the risk that the enquiry would extend embarrassingly into the whole working of the capitalist system". That was not the sort of inquiry or investigative reporting that the Tories were keen to encourage.

However, MacMillan accepted that there was a case for "an enquiry into the economics of the newspaper industry and, more particularly, into the restrictive practices of the trades unions concerned". He also made clear that this attack on union power in the print should be done in an underhand way. "It would, however, be preferable that the terms of reference [of the Royal Commission] should not make any explicit mention of the relationship between management and labour."[11] Days later MacMillan announced the second Royal Commission on the press to pursue those aims, under the guise of an inquiry into standards and regulation.

The Conservative government agreed to launch that inquiry as an underhand assault on "the restrictive practices of the trade unions" in the print. Are we to imagine that the Tories would have appeared so concerned about the standards of the British press if their pals in the industry had not been in such a state of financial crisis, and if the print unions had not resisted cost-cutting reform of working methods?

These examples from recent history of how particular agendas and interests always underlie general concerns about press standards surely ought to raise other questions. Why should we accept at face value the complaints about press immorality, intrusion or privacy that have been expressed so loudly of late, notably through the Leveson Inquiry into the "ethics and culture" of the media? Are we innocent enough to imagine that, for the first time in modern history, the British authorities would have set up an investigation into the press for purely altruistic and "ethical" motives, with no axe to grind against any section of the media? Is it too cynical to suggest that those who whisper conspiratorially about the "dark arts" of the popular media and the "secret state" run by the Murdoch press might have some (barely-)hidden motives of their own?

It is remarkable that the parade of celebrities, politicians and public figures leading the ethical charge have been allowed to present themselves as noble champions of the public interest, despite all having personal scores to settle with the tabloid press. Indeed the high-minded sections of the media and academia that are normally so sniffy about low celebrity culture embraced the actors, comedians and others starring at the Leveson Inquiry like teenagers in thrall to pop stars. Former Labour deputy prime minister John Prescott, whose anti-Murdoch campaign is naturally in no way connected to the humiliation the tabloids caused him over his affair with his secretary, appears to have been transformed in the upmarket media's eyes from national laughing stock to almost a national hero.

Nobody involved in this debate has a disinterested view of the press. Everybody has a stake in one side or another in the battle over regulation and reform. Those who claim that they are above all that and are simply interested in creating a cleaner media for our children to enjoy should be scoffed at as loudly and questioned as closely as a proprietor who claims he is not in it to make money.

We might start by questioning more closely the language that has come to dominate the discussion of the press around phone-hacking and Leveson. The need to uphold "ethical journalism" and defend "the public interest" is repeatedly cited to justify attacks on the tabloid press and to distinguish the quality, liberal media from the mob. They are joined together by media academics, experts and campaigners to raise the sacred ideal of "ethical public-interest journalism". Thus Hacked Off, the lobby group at the centre of pursuing the phone-hacking scandal, demands that Leveson should result in "a system of press regulation which affords the maximum freedom for ethical journalism in the public interest while bearing down on journalism which breaches accepted professional codes of practice".[12]

That all sounds well and good. But can these concepts of ethical journalism and the public interest be quite as black-and-white or unquestionable as they have been made to appear? What do they mean in practice for the press, and the public?

"What is Truth?"

In expressing to Lord Justice Leveson his uncertainty about what "ethical" might mean, the press/porn baron Richard Desmond inadvertently pointed up an inconvenient truth: that there is no consensus on ethics in society. There is more than one idea of morality in the world, depending on where you stand.

Take a question as fundamental as war and peace. When almost any war is threatened or launched these days, you can expect to hear an avowedly moral case being made both for and against the conflict. For some, the US-UK invasion of Iraq in 2003 was a moral mission to counter the Hitlerian evil of Saddam Hussein. For others it was a wicked scheme to grab Iraqi oil reserves. (Some of us did not entirely swallow either of those arguments, demonstrating that just because something can be said to be ethical does not necessarily make it convincing.) It is the same story of competing ethical pros and cons with most issues that divide opinion—and that can mean almost any issue in our age when the moral consensus of old has broken down on questions ranging from gay marriage to wind farms. Which moral argument you accept as right and true depends which side you are on.

The definition of what is considered ethical practice by the press also changes with time and circumstances. One study of the issues of ethical journalism, for example, points out that in 1954, the initial report of the General Council of the Press (set up after the first Royal Commission) discussed the problem that "reports of [court] proceedings against homosexual suspects caused some public protests", presumably because some readers thought it immoral to mention such distasteful matters. The Council decided that, so long as there was no "indecent mention of physiological details" of what the "homosexual suspects" got up to, the reports were morally justified because "If a great evil is rife in our midst, the facts should be made known".[13] Any writer using the word "indecent", never mind "evil", to describe homosexual matters today would immediately find themselves in the dock for unethical journalism. As far back as 1990 the Press Council ruled that the words "poof and poofter" were "so offensive to male homosexuals that publishing them is not a matter of taste or opinion within a newspaper editor's discretion".

When it comes to matters of taste and decency, what is considered right to do and to report changes with time and place. Nor is the meaning of privacy any easier to define for all occasions—worth remembering when some are trying to present their preferred rules against intrusion as ageless ethical norms. As the Oxford don Terry Eagleton has pointed out, for example, "Nothing in human life is inherently private. Certainly not urinating, defecating and copulating, which only a few centuries ago could be performed in public with no sense of shame. Bedrooms were not particularly private places in medieval Europe, and wanting to relieve yourself unobserved might be considered as eccentric as wanting to crack jokes in utter solitude".[14] The idea of institutionalising a fixed catch-all definition of taste, decency, privacy or other "ethical" matters is as historically ignorant as it is culturally naïve.

The claim of ethical journalism has long been used as a sort of class divide to separate those who work in the "quality" press and upper end of the media from lowly tabloid hacks. The first codes of conduct for journalists were introduced in the nineteenth century in the USA, and then in the UK, precisely to set responsible reporters apart from the "yellow press". When the National Union of Journalists passed its first code in 1936, some members objected on the grounds that ethics ought to be left to individual judgement. Others wanted to go further; the NUJ's rival, the Institute of Journalists, proposed the introduction of a register for professional scribes, from which unethical reporters could effectively be struck off—a divisive plan for the official licensing of journalists that we heard echoed by academics and even some journalists around the Leveson Inquiry.

Is it so straightforward, however, to draw a timeless, absolute line between the decent and the indecent in journalism? Those who insist on the need for such a rigid ethical code from the clouds to regulate the press today are pursuing their own meaning of ethics, that is no more impartial than Richard Desmond's—except they hide theirs in more highfalutin language. The constant talk of ethical journalism has become the natural language of the "press freedom, BUT…" lobby. Yes they believe in a free press, but only really for those who fit their "ethical" bill. The key thing is the implication that journalists who differ from them—that "different breed" or "other species" —are inherently unethical. The Coordinating Committee for Media Reform, a lobby group of academics, writers and activists, observes that journalism is now "sharply divided" between those who "operate ethically" and those who will do it "by any means possible". In other words, it's ethical "us" against unethical "them".[15]

Really? There are different types of newspaper and media outlet with different aims, modus operandi and audiences. But the idea that this is a moral divide sounds like sanctimonious snobbery. Any paper or news outlet is capable of getting carried away with itself in pursuit of its pet stories. Tabloids can certainly be accused of getting stories "by any means possible". Sometimes their methods might appear justified—think of the *News of the World*'s genuine exposés of royal sleaze or sporting corruption—sometimes not. But what of the other side?

Where, for example, was the broadsheet press "operating ethically" in 2008, when it splashed sensational horror stories about child murders at a children's home on Jersey, with headlines such as "Six more bodies feared buried in Jersey home" which turned out to be based on little more than the discovery of some ancient bones and a piece of coconut?[16] What was ethical about the disgraceful scare-stories erroneously linking the MMR triple vaccination to autism which ran in the UK press for a decade from 1998, doing untold harm to children's health? This baseless panic originated not in the tabloid press but in the leading medical journal *The Lancet*, and outlets which consistently gave it headline credence included not only the tabloid *Daily Mail* but broadsheets such as the *Sunday Telegraph*—and the satirical journal *Private Eye*, which normally loves to look down upon the low morals and paranoia of the tabloid press.[17]

Or what about the ethics of the "quality" media publishing celebrity gossip as news? Asked about this dubious area of journalism at the Leveson Inquiry, one editor suggested that, while his paper did not go after such stories, they did have to follow up and comment on what the rest of the media was reporting, such as the tales of golfer Tiger Woods' infidelity. So is it unethical to break celebrity gossip stories, but ethical to go in for sloppy seconds?

One indisputable ethical standard for journalists ought surely to be the requirement to tell the truth, a moral absolute if ever there was one. As I tell the students I meet at the Young Journalists Academy each summer, no self-respecting journalist should willingly put their name to something they know to be untrue. The truth is attainable through rigorous investigation, critical analysis and honest argument, and should not be knowingly sacrificed to corner-cutting expediency.

Yet even the issue of truth is not always as set in ethical stone as one might assume. After all, each of us can only testify to the truth *as we understand it*. Witnesses on both sides in a court case will swear to tell the whole truth before relating their contrasting stories; it is then left to the jury to decide which one is true. Journalists do the same before a jury of their peers—the public. Those viewing events from different viewpoints may see the truth very differently. They might be watching the same match, for instance, and repeatedly viewing the same slow-motion replays of the incident. Yet no two football pundits, let alone rival supporters, ever seem likely to agree on the truth of whether or not it was a penalty.

The problem of competing views of the truth is clear in another area that is even more important than football—politics. In 2010 the former Labour minister Phil Woolas was disqualified as an MP by an electoral court for allegedly telling lies about his Lib Dem opponent in election literature and press statements. Woolas's response was that "I did not peddle falsehoods. Everything I did was to do with politics". He has a point. Democratic politics is traditionally a dirty business, elections a fight to the finish between hostile camps. This is a struggle for power, not a polite dinner party. To win, all sides will seek to paint their opponents in the worst possible light. Outright lies rarely have an impact on the public—the electorate is too sophisticated for that. However, exaggerations and caricatures that bear some relation to public perceptions of reality, with a bit of invective thrown in, are pretty much par for the course. Is politics always to be condemned outright as unethical?[18]

One aspect of journalism that raises important questions about the pursuit of the truth is the role of eye-witnesses. Eye-witness accounts by reporters on the ground are much prized in the modern media. They are felt to give a story authenticity and humanity that colder, more distant analysis lacks. Some reporters pride themselves on writing "the first draft of history".

There will be more to say in a later section about the problem of journalists putting themselves at the centre of the story and potentially confusing a subjective, emotive reaction with a search for the objective facts. For now, however, it is worth unearthing the views of the veteran British writer Malcolm Muggeridge. In an essay written almost 50 years ago entitled "The Eye-witness Fallacy", Muggeridge observed that "It is sad to reflect that the more reputable the eye-witness, the greater the caution with which his testimony should be received… Out of righteousness and sincerity have come more deception than out of villainy and deliberate deceit. The tabloid press, with many readers, deludes few. Serious newspapers like *The Times* and the *Guardian*, with fewer readers, delude many… I find it difficult to see how truth could ever be extracted from this plethora of eye-witnesses, whose ostensible credentials are so impressive, but whose testimony is so dubious… It is not surprising that Pontius Pilate did not wait for an answer when he asked his famous question, 'What is truth?' He, too, had doubtless been studying eye-witnesses' reports, including, of course, that of Judas Iscariot".[19]

I have no interest in indulging the nonsense of post-modern relativism. Contrary to that lamentable excuse for a theory, truth can be established and it can be absolute—at least for now. Journalists should always seek it without fear or favour, and never ignore it because it does not suit their story. The point is, however, that the search to understand the truth is often a difficult mission through a minefield of messy facts, competing arguments, conflicting eyewitness accounts and contextual analyses. A journalist negotiating that minefield needs to keep his wits about him and his value judgements sharpened — rather than trying to rely on a black-and-white ethical map imposed from the outside on fast-changing terrain.

The truth is to be scrapped for and fought over using whatever methods are deemed necessary in the circumstances. It cannot always simply be handed down from on high by ethically-approved journalists carrying the revealed Word of Wikileaks inscribed on their (digital) tablets. What is more, once something is accepted as the truth it must still be open to challenge and question at every turn. To suggest that something is "beyond question" on moral grounds, or that a debate is "closed" and that scepticism is somehow unethical, flies in the face of the traditional liberal attitude, as outlined by J.S. Mill. Truth, insisted Mill, was not something to be assumed or accepted as beyond challenge, but to be tested through argument at every opportunity. "There is the greatest difference", he observed, "between presuming an opinion to be true because, with every opportunity for contesting it, it has not been refuted, and assuming its truth for the purpose of not permitting its refutation."[20] The best way to the truth lies always through more freedom of expression and questioning everything, not further restrictions and regulation, however they might be justified.

What About the Moral Case for a Free Press?

Once you get beyond something as specific as not hacking the phones of missing teenagers, and something as general as telling the truth, a one-size-fits-all definition of ethical journalism can prove elusive. Instead it becomes clearer that all the talk of high-level over-arching ethics can be a cover for trying to impose a particular code of conduct on all parts of the press whether they like it or not.

In many fields of academia and social policy, the ethics industry is a booming concern these days. Talking about ethical standards and codes is often a way of justifying the management and policing of other people's affairs, masquerading as a philosophical and moral point of view. Experts and authorities will hide behind the idea of ethics, to find some transcendental principle to justify themselves. An apparently ethereal ethics becomes a sort of *deus-ex-machina* through which to impose one viewpoint over others. The discussion of ethical journalism is no exception to this trend.

One thing gives the game away in relation to the press: that what is presented as the "ethical" case always appears to be the one for less freedom, for bringing the press and particularly the tabloids under closer control. Strange how demands presented in the language of ethics always turn out to be for new laws and statute-backed regulation, for legal definitions of the public interest and tighter rules on what can be done. As that academic guide to ethical journalism mentioned above puts it, "There is a close relationship between the law and ethics, as both are attempting to restrain or constrain the media to act responsibly".[21] It seems that the supposedly ethical case is always the conservative one, the illiberal argument. Ethics is the "BUT" at the end of the debate about press freedom.

But... what about the moral case for a freer press? If you believe, as I do, in a human-centred morality, there can be no higher moral good than freedom of expression. The right to live as a morally autonomous individual has to involve the freedom to think and speak as you see fit — and just as importantly, the freedom to hear all the arguments and choose for yourself. Those fundamental liberties of a human-centred society do not appear to feature in the prescriptive demands for more ethics in the media. It is high time the moral arguments for a free and open press were shouted from the mountain.

Instead we are faced with a situation where the demand for "ethical journalism" is always apparently an argument for more control of the press, or even censorship. In January 2012 the former Labour minister and anti-pornography crusader Clare

Short wrote a column in the *Independent* insisting that, if he was serious about improving "media ethics", Lord Justice Leveson should do what she had failed to do, and banish Page 3 pin-ups from the tabloid press. In a fine display of one-eyed double-standards, Short declared that the press had conspired to "censor public debate" — about her campaign to, err, get the government to censor the press by banning Page 3. You do not have to be a fan of topless photos in newspapers to question how, in the name of "media ethics", censorship can somehow be turned into its opposite. Some might call that naked opportunism.[22]

So much for the false idol of ethical journalism. Let us turn to the other totemic demand of the "press freedom, but…" lobby: that journalism should be properly free only if pursued in "the public interest".

Where are the Public in the "Public Interest"?

Everybody loves journalism pursued "in the public interest". It is an unquestionable Good Thing, another mom and apple pie issue. No wonder every journalist and publication likes to summon up the public interest to support their case. Once you look into matters a little closer, however, the virtues of journalism justified "in the public interest" seem slightly more open to question than those of motherhood or home-baked fruit desserts. The key questions being, as the legal counsel to the Leveson Inquiry posed them in his opening statement: what exactly do we mean by "the public interest", and who is to define it?

The answers to these questions appeared to be: it will be left to the likes of Lord Justice Leveson and his judicial ilk to define the public interest for the press, with advice from a fan club in the upper circles of the legal, political, media and celebrity worlds. The one section of society who will definitely not get a say in deciding what is in the public interest will be the public, the democratic majority.

Some campaigners for press reform and firmer regulation are now calling for the public interest to be clearly defined in UK law. That way, they suggest, it could be applied by judges both to offer legal protection to quality, ethical journalists who act in the public interest, and to punish those unethical journalists who merely pretend to do so. One journalism professor argued at a Westminster forum on press regulation that the public interest could be defined in law "absolutely, the same way that murder is defined in law, there are problems, you know, and that's what courts are there to determine".[23]

Good luck with that. Any attempt to give a clear legal definition of the public interest that could cover all eventualities might succeed in providing a lot of well-paid work for lawyers and parliamentary drafters. It seems unlikely to do anybody else much good.

In celebrity privacy suits and similar cases brought before the courts in recent years, various judges have often appeared to interpret "the public interest" to mean quite different things in different circumstances. As one lawyer noted in a case back in 1990, "the so-called public interest defence is not so much a rule of law as an invitation to judicial idiosyncrasy".[24] Those murky legal waters have been further muddied by the passage of the Human Rights Act, which has written into law both the right to privacy and the right to freedom of expression, hence creating endless scope for legal chancers and institutionalising a standing feast for lawyers and judges.

Like the concept of "ethical journalism", the notion of the public interest turns out in practice to be less of a universal value than a cover for pursuing what are really matters of taste, preference and personal interest.

Take the example of quality newspapers such as the *Guardian* and the *Daily Telegraph* in the UK, and the *New York Times* in the USA, publishing high-end gossip that they extracted from the Wikileaks files, which that outfit had in turn gained by underhand and sometimes illegal methods. How did that differ from the *News of the World* publishing low-level gossip obtained by other underhand and sometimes illegal methods including, we now know, phone-hacking?

There did not always seem to be that much difference in the nature of the content. We learned from the Wikileaks extracts in the quality press, for example, that the then-dictator of Libya, Colonel Gaddafi, used botox and lusted after his Ukrainian nurse; that the then-dictator of North Korea, Kim il Jung, had a weight problem and was considered "flabby"; and that the then-president of France, Nicolas Sarkozy, was a rude, "thin-skinned authoritarian" who when he wasn't throwing his sleight weight around his office once chased a pet dog and rabbit around it. All fascinating stuff no doubt, and not at all the type of thing one might read in a gossip sheet.

What, then, was the difference? It was obvious, explained the *Guardian*'s media correspondent: "The whole point about the *News of the World*'s phone hacking is that the stories it obtained could not be said to have been in the public interest, [whereas] we can demonstrate that we are acting in the public interest."[25] Let us understand: it was not in the public interest for the *NotW* to reveal Prince Harry's embarrassing private conversation with his girlfriend Chelsy about his visit to a strip club. But it was in the public interest for the *Guardian* to reveal that Prince Andrew spoke "cockily" and embarrassingly at a private function in America? (He apparently criticised "****ing journalists" from the broadsheet press, which may be the definition of infringing the public interest in some eyes.) Glad we were able to clear that up.

This sounds more like a question of taste or even of snob-bery — "our gossip is more ethical than your gossip" — rather than an all-purpose definition of the public interest. In fact the editor of the *Guardian* rather spelt out the partial character of his "public interest" defence in relation to the Wikileaks revelations. He explained that he and a select team of his most senior journalists — those with "great knowledge" — had been through the diplomatic documents leaked by Wikileaks to work out which of them it would be "in the public interest" to publish.

But how did they know? Where did the wise men of the newsroom gain this "great knowledge" of what is and is not in the public interest? Given the humanist pretensions of the paper, it seems unlikely they would claim it was God-given wisdom. Instead, the documents these half-dozen senior broadsheet journalists deemed to be in the public interest were presumably the ones they wanted published. Had it been half-a-dozen tabloid journalists doing the choosing, they may have opted to publish a different selection of juicy political titbits. Whether their personal choice would have been any more or less "in the public interest", however, remains very much open to question. You pays your money for the paper you prefer and takes your choice (or not).

One thing for certain amid all this confusion is that it will not be left to the public to decide what is in the public interest. But then, what did the concept of the "public interest" ever have to do with them?

Even when it was first coined in the eighteenth century, the "public interest" was conceived by political elites as a device for keeping the passions of the actual breathing public in check. After the American people had won their revolutionary war against the British Crown, some among the leaders of the newly-independent USA became concerned about the unruly popular potential that had been unleashed. In *The Federalist Papers* of the late 1780s, written to ratify and to rein in the republicanism of the American Constitution, James Madison sought to identify a "public interest" that would exist some-where above the desires of the American people. His hope was that a "public interest" identified and upheld by relatively few "enlightened citizens" could help to guard against the excesses of the "fickleness and passion" of the public, that "overbearing majority".[26]

That idea of an officially-endorsed "public interest", stand-ing above and separate from the madding crowd below, has been developed by political elites over the past 200 years to help control what information and influence the public should be allowed to access, down here on Earth. Today, the British public are still apparently to be excluded from decisions as to what might be in the public interest.

The mood in the current discussion of the public interest was best captured by Hugh Grant, as voiceover artist for the tabloid-bashing lobby, giving evidence to the Leveson Inquiry after being well-briefed by his lawyer friends. Who, he asked, "is better to decide whether a piece of journalism is in the public interest or not? Would that be a judge, or would it be the tabloid editor who stands to profit commercially from the piece?"[27] So that's our choice, apparently. The "public interest" is to be decided either by a venal tabloid editor, or by a venerable member of the bench. Either way it will be an internal elite affair, decided in the courtroom, from which the public are barred. Not surprisingly, the press reform lobby goes with the judge making the decision and imposing injunctions on miscreant newspapers. The fact that an unelected judge is even less accountable to the public than a tabloid editor, who at least has to relate to his readers, only makes that option more attractive to those whose hatred of the tabloid press is a thinly-disguised loathing of those who read it.

The point that is always being made, over and again, is that "the public interest" is not the same thing as that which interests the public. In other words, just because the public might want to see or read something, does not mean they should be allowed to do so — it may well be in "the public interest" to curb the interest of the public. This "the public interest, not what interests the public" line has become such a repetitive chant that nobody seems to question it anymore.

Yet what does it really mean? Such an uber-patronising approach suggests that the public cannot appreciate what is in its own best interests. That the mass of people do not know what is good for them to know. Therefore the elites must remove the public from the public interest, and possibly remove what they are interested in from the public arena. Instead, an enlightened clique of judges and experts must be left to define the public interest on the public's behalf. It's for our own good. And they must do so in such a way as to limit exposure to the public of material that is not in the public interest. In short the elite must stick another "But" on the end of press freedom, this time in the name of the public interest.

As one journalism academic says, if the tabloid press were allowed to get away with publishing gossip and scandal in the public's name, "it will not be what we understand as the public interest".[28] Who is this "we" of whom he speaks, who have apparently monopolised the proper understanding of the public interest? For "we" read the experts, academics and "ethical" media people who are founding members of the "press freedom, but..." club.

By now it is becoming clear that the "public interest", far from being a general ethical standard, is another device for interest groups to express a particular view of the press and freedom of expression—one that often seems to view the tabloids as essentially not fit to be published.

It was striking, during his opening statement to Leveson, to hear counsel to the Inquiry Robert Jay complain that "the public interest is very often deployed as some form of trump card" by the tabloids to justify "delving" into the affairs of celebrities and others which "unethically penetrates" their privacy. No doubt that has often been true. Today, however, the "public interest" is also being "deployed as some sort of trump card" by the tabloid-bashing lobby for more rigorous press regulation. They will wheel it out when it suits to blow away any opposition. To disagree with them becomes to go against the public interest and commit a crime against ethical journalism.[29]

Whether these more-ethical-than-thou guardians of the public interest like it or not, however, the problem remains that questions to do with public taste and sensibilities cannot properly be micro-managed in advance by a general decree or codes of conduct. Not even Lord Justice Leveson and his chorus of legal and celebrity angels are capable of handing down commandments set in stone, to instruct us as to the true meaning of "ethical public-interest journalism" now and in the news hereafter. Any attempt to do so can only create more confusion and conformity by imposing one view of the Good Media over all others.

Unsurprisingly it has proved far easier to hold forth about defining the public interest than to do so in practice and in law. In February 2012 the Director of Public Prosecutions, Kier Starmer, promised the Leveson Inquiry that he would address the problem of clearly defining the public interest. In April, with 40 people on bail on allegations of phone-hacking and other press-related offences, he issued guidelines which, as the *Independent* observed, "singularly fail to do that...We cannot duck the issue, he said. That is precisely what he has done". Yet the paper admitted through its evident frustration, "that may be for the best".

What the DPP effectively conceded was that it is better for the authorities to judge each of "these sensitive and difficult cases" involving the media on its individual merits, rather than trying to apply some general definition of the public interest. He acknowledged that recent decisions not to prosecute journalists and their sources who used questionable means to break stories —such as *The Telegraph* and the MPs' expenses claims—would stand under the new guidelines. That is good news of course. Yet in suggesting that journalistic criminality might be outweighed by public interest considerations where the media are "raising or contributing to an important matter of public debate", the new guidelines only point up the question: who is to decide what is important to public debate? The *Independent* concluded that "the old maxim about the public interest not being the same as what interests the public is just given new impetus". And that is surely not such good news for the public at all.[30]

It is time to question the very language used in this discussion, to reject any notion that there is a "public interest" that is somehow separate from the actual public, and which can be decided or defined by a committee or a court sitting on an ethereal, ethical cloud. In the end, the question of what sort of press coverage best serves the public's interests can only be decided in the particular context of events. More importantly, it can ultimately only be decided by the public.

This is the other non-negotiable aspect of a free press and freedom of expression. It must involve not only the freedom to say or write what you believe, but also the liberty to watch, listen to or read what you choose. It is the freedom to think and judge for yourself. That is a freedom which belongs not to a few editors or experts or law lords, but to the democratic mass of readers, viewers and listeners.

In a free society the public must be allowed to decide for itself what interests it, and what it deems to be in its interest to know. How are people to make such a judgement? Not by being instructed what to think by judges, as jurors find they often are. The public must be allowed openly to consider all of the evidence, as a free jury should be. In other words the public cannot know what is in its interests until it has a basis to decide, after everything is laid out before it. The freedom of the press to publish cannot be dependent on a pre-definition of the public interest in regulations or the law. On the contrary: the public can only decide after publication, when all sides of the argument are out in the open and competing in the public arena. At which point we should all be free to endorse, argue against, embrace, ignore, boycott or shout "bullshit!" at what is published, as we see fit in our role as public arbiters. But not to go running to the regulators or the courts to have the publication punished in "the public interest".

Of course, the sort of stories for which the tabloids are best known may not serve any higher purpose. But we can only have a debate about issues such as privacy by having it all out in the open. In any case, it is not for judges or others to decide what is fit for somebody to publish. Even if something does not fit through the high and narrow entrance into "public interest journalism", so what? People should still be at liberty to publish and be judged by the public. Even those who we might think are wrong have the right to be heard.

If some still insist that we come up with a suitably pretentious-sounding definition of the public interest, perhaps we might settle for something like: the greatest public interest is served by the greatest possible freedom of expression. And we should pass judgement on anybody who appears to have an interest in limiting that liberty, even — or especially — if they excuse their action in the name of the public interest.

For those of us who believe in a free press, the cloak of "the public interest" is becoming a contender for public enemy number one.

1   Richard Desmond at the Leveson Inquiry, 12 January 2012
    (http://www.levesoninquiry.org.uk/wp-content/uploads/2012/
    01/Transcript-of-Afternoon-Hearing-12-January-2012.txt).
2   Quoted in the *Daily Mail*, 7 December 2011.
3   Quoted in the *Daily Mail*, 24 January 2012.
4   Onora O'Neill, 'The rights of journalism and the needs of audiences',
    Reuters Memorial Lecture, November 2011 (http://reutersinstitute.
    politics.ox.ac.uk/fileadmin/documents/presentations/The_Rights_
    of_Journalism_and_Needs_of_Audiences.pdf).
5   W.T. Stead, 'Notice to our readers: a frank warning', *Pall Mall
    Gazette*, 4 July 1885 (http://www.attackingthedevil.co.uk/pmg/
    tribute/notice.php); 'The maiden tribute of modern Babylon part I:
    the report of our secret commission', *Pall Mall Gazette*, 6 July 1885
    (http://www.attackingthedevil.co.uk/pmg/tribute/mt1.php).
6   *The Times*, 19 January 2012.
7   William Randolph Hearst, 1863–1951, cited in http://thinkexist.
    com/quotes/william_randolph_hearst/
8   The *Guardian*, 23 November 2011.
9   See Brendan O'Neill, 'Using tabloid tactics to slay the tabloids',
    Spiked, 3 January 2012 (http://www.spiked-online.com/site/
    article/11946/).
10 Tom O'Malley and Clive Soley, *Regulating the Press*, Pluto 2000, pp.
    52–53.
11 *Ibid.*, p. 62.
12 *Hacked Off Manifesto*, http://hackinginquiry.org/news/hacked-off-
    manifesto/
13 Cited in Chris Frost, *Journalism Ethics and Regulation*, Longman
    Practical Journalism 2011, p. 228.
14 The *Guardian*, 28 November 2011.
15 Coordinating Committee for Media Reform, 'Promoting a demo-
    cratic and accountable media', in *The Phone-Hacking Scandal: Journal-
    ism on Trial*, p. 345.
16 The *Guardian*, 25 February 2008; see Mick Hume, 'No murder at the
    mansion', *The Times*, 16 December 2008.
17 See Dr Michael Fitzpatrick, 'The death agony of the anti-MMR
    campaign', *Spiked*, 11 November 2005 (http://spiked-online.
    com/Articles/0000000CAE57.htm); and 'Turning a blind eye to the
    truth', *Spiked*, 1 March 2010 (http://www.spiked-online.com/index.
    php/site/article/8257/).
18 Quoted in *The Asian News*, 15 September 2010 (http://menmedia.co.
    uk/asiannews/news/s/1324973_phil_woolas_complains_of_vicious
    _campaign).
19 Malcolm Muggeridge, *Tread Softly, For You Tread on My Jokes*, Collins

1966, p. 75.

[20] J.S. Mill, *On Liberty*, Chapter 2 'Of the liberty of thought and discussion', Oxford World Classics 1998 edition, p. 24.

[21] Frost, *Journalism Ethics and Regulation*, p. 210.

[22] The *Independent*, 26 January 2012.

[23] Professor Steven Barnett at Westminster Media Forum, 'Priorities for press regulation', 26 March 2012.

[24] Cited in Frost, *Journalism Ethics and Regulation*, p. 113.

[25] *Media Guardian*, 1 December 2010.

[26] James Madison, *The Federalist Papers*, http://www.foundingfathers.info/federalistpapers/madison.htm

[27] Hugh Grant at the Leveson Inquiry, 21 November 2011 (http://www.levesoninquiry.org.uk/wp-content/uploads/2011/11/Transcript-of-Afternoon-Hearing-21-November-2011.txt).

[28] Phil Harding, 'Journalism in the public interest', in *The Phone-Hacking Scandal: Journalism on Trial*, p. 311.

[29] Robert Jay QC, opening submission to Leveson Inquiry, 14 November 2011 (http://www.levesoninquiry.org.uk/wp-content/uploads/2011/12/Transcript-of-Morning-Hearing-14-November-2011.txt).

[30] The *Independent*, 19 April 2012.

Chapter Three

Fear and Loathing of the Popular

How did "popular" become a dirty word? The more innocent among us might assume that to be popular would generally be thought a good thing, a mark of approval, or at least preferable to its opposite. Yet when it comes to discussing the media, "popular" turns into a boo-word. The "popular press" is a phrase generally pronounced with a sneer and a good deal of spittle on the "p"s. The term is intended to imply that the best-selling tabloids are low, cheap, vulgar, vulgar, vulgar.

Why should "popular" assume such a pejorative meaning in the eyes of media-watchers? Perhaps the word's origins can provide a clue. It comes, the *Collins English Dictionary* reminds us, "from the Latin *popularis,* belonging to the people, democratic, from *populus,* people".

There we have it, the secret is out. The cultural elite despise the "popular press" not simply because of phone-hacking scandals or Page 3 pin-ups. They despise the tabloids because they are of the masses, "belonging to the people" in spirit if not of course in law; "democratic" at least in the broadest, non-political sense of *demos,* the people. "Popular" is here a code word for the fear and loathing that dare not speak its name — contempt for the populace. If they were being honest, the cultural elitists might as well call it the prole press, the downstairs press, the filthy press of the great unwashed. Except that they do not have the nerve. So "popular" has become a popular euphemism in those circles.

Here is another unspoken truth of the debate about press reform. The disdain expressed towards tabloid or "popular" newspapers and the "mass media" is at root a reflection of the contempt felt for the people who consume and sometimes even enjoy them.

The mass of readers who put the populace in the popular press are the true targets of the venom. They, after all, are the ones who fund and sustain it. They are the ones who line the likes of Rupert Murdoch's pockets. They are the ones whose "vulgar" tastes dictate the contents of the papers. And they are the ones supposedly stupid enough to allow themselves to be "duped" by tabloid propaganda into voting Tory, or hating asylum-seekers, or loving *The Only Way is Get Me Out of The X Factor on Ice*. Off with their headlines!

Many of those who express a wish to regulate the press more strictly would really like to regulate the thoughts and deeds of the mass of readers. But in these allegedly enlightened times, it is not considered acceptable publicly to defecate on millions of "ordinary people". Gone are the days when it was deemed legitimate for the upper orders to address the lower ones as council estate scum or ordure-eating peasants fit only for horse-whipping.

What you can do, however, is to signal the moral inferiority of the masses by lambasting the standards of the media that they consume. When you get to the bottom of it, many criticisms of tabloid journalism, the "popular" press, the "mass" media, news-as-entertainment and all rest of it, have become the permissible way for the cultural elite to look down on the people, by separating the habits of the sophisticated few from those of the herd.

It is a neat trick. The fire in this culture war can all ostensibly be aimed at such rich and powerful hate-figures as Rupert Murdoch, or love-hate figures such as Simon Cowell, or at the editors and apparatchiks they employ. Media moguls can even be blasted by critics claiming to act in the name of "ordinary people". But the subterranean attack is on the mass audience of "sheeple" who these Svengali-like super-villains allegedly manipulate and milk at will.

What, after all, do the high-minded critics most often claim is wrong with the mass media? One central complaint is that the tabloids and their television equivalents are driven to excess by the "commercial pressures" of the market place. That line might seem appealing to an old Marxist such as me. But what does it really mean? Are they offering a critique of the political economy of capitalism? Not quite.

Instead what the critics usually mean is that the popular press is "pandering" to the mass market—that is, selling people what they want. The implication is that Murdoch's *Sun*, the *Mail*, *Star* and the rest are essentially stooping to the taste level of the masses in order to conquer the market. In which case, it must be the crass punters who are ultimately to blame for what are deemed to be the media's crimes against culture.

Of course the ostensible target in the culture war is Big Media rather than the masses. The underlying assumption, however, is always that the former has tailored or "dumbed down" its content in order to exploit the gullibility and base tastes of the latter.

Look at the debate about politics and the media, and the argument that the tabloids have been responsible for deciding the outcome of British elections—a patronising notion which the politicians themselves often seem to believe. Perhaps the most famous illustration was the consensus that it was "The *Sun* wot won it", after John Major's Tories confounded many pundits and pollsters by defeating Neil Kinnock's Labour Party in the general election of 1992. Everybody from the Labour leader himself to the BBC seemed to accept that a single *Sun* front page, warning that "If Kinnock wins today, will the last person to leave Britain please turn out the lights?" had turned millions of voters away from Labour and denied Kinnock his rightful triumph at the polls. It couldn't have been that the *Sun* was simply reflecting the lack of faith in Kinnock's flailing Labour Party among intelligent voters, could it?

If anything these prejudices about the political influence of the mass media over the gullible masses run even deeper 20 years later. In March 2012 the Left-wing maverick George Galloway shocked the Westminster set by coming from nowhere to win a parliamentary by-election in Bradford West, turning a 5,000-vote Labour majority into a 10,000 majority for his small Respect Party. How to explain this dramatic upheaval? What might it tell us about the crisis of the traditional parties? A Labour MP from a neighbouring constituency was in no doubt: it was Celebrity Big Brother wot won it.

Toby Perkins MP insisted that Galloway's notorious appearance on the reality TV show back in 2006 had been a "very significant factor" in getting people to vote for him six years later: "I think frankly there wasn't a lot the other parties could do about it. They had seen him on [Celebrity] Big Brother. They wanted him on their streets and now they've got him."[1] Leave aside for a moment the small fact that Galloway's risible appearance on *CBB*, crawling around the floor in a red catsuit unflattering to the fuller figure, was widely considered to spell the end of his political career. The idea that people are sheeple who will vote for whoever they see on reality TV, leaving political parties helpless to turn back the tide of celeb-obsessed ignorance, summed up the mixture of incomprehension and contempt with which the political elite views the masses today.

The common complaints about "manipulative" media advertising carry the same "hidden message" about the idiot masses. The demands from health campaigners for a UK ban on the advertising of fast food or alcohol, and government steps to remove cigarettes from public display and confine them to plain packaging, are presented as attacks on the corporate giants of Big Food, Big Booze or Big Tobacco. But the ultimate target is always the Big Public, seen as so gullible and gormless that it can be turned into a wheezing mass of obese alcoholics if allowed a glimpse of a Big Mac or a Bacardi bottle on the TV, or exposed to the siren call of a brightly coloured fag packet in the corner shop. The campaign to curb Big Media advertising

ʿuttles common consumers as if we were infants incapable of making our own choices.

At best the highbrow critics complain that television is "dumbing down" by pandering to low public tastes in soaps and "reality" TV shows. (In fact such programmes usually say more about the prejudices of TV producers than the public.) At worst, they warn that the media is "playing with fire" by stoking up fear and hatred of Islam, asylum-seekers, homosexuals, the disabled or Cheryl Cole. All of these ostensible criticisms of the mass media are barely-disguised expressions of disgust with the not-so-great British public, who are viewed from above as a bear-baiting mob and a pogrom waiting to happen, a pile of brainless firewood waiting for a spark from an inflammatory newspaper.

Two issues discussed at the Leveson Inquiry illustrated the contempt for the public that lies behind concerns over "media culture". First, a group of feminist lobbyists turned up to complain to Lord Justice Leveson about Page 3, as part of their campaign to get the government to ban those famous tabloid pin-ups. Their objection was not simply that they found such images distasteful to look at; after all, it seems doubtful that they ever touch a copy of the *Sun* or the *Daily Star*. The radical feminists' deeper concern was over the impact these pin-ups have on the blighted male—and female—readers of those papers. According to one of the lobby groups, Page 3 snaps are "encouraging and endorsing negative attitudes towards us and within us, and at worst, acts of violence committed against us. All of which grossly limit our choices, stall our progress and violate our human rights".[2] Blimey. But how could some silly snaps of young models with their tops off be held responsible for discrimination, human rights violations and possibly even sexual violence against women? Only if you believe that male readers of the popular press are such thick bigots that they can be turned into rights-abusers and even rapists by the sight of a printed nipple over breakfast. And also that women exposed to the tabloids are such pathetic creatures that they can be reduced to self-loathing jelly "within us" by the thought of a photo of somebody else's breasts. The radical campaign to ban Page 3 rests upon some familiar conservative prejudices about the people who read the other pages of the tabloid press.

Then came a little-noticed exchange about paedophiles between Robert Jay, the lead lawyer at the Leveson Inquiry, and Rebekah Brooks, the former editor of the *Sun* and the *News of the World* and ex-chief executive of News International. In 2000, in support of the Sunday paper's campaign for "Sarah's Law", to allow the public to identify known sex offenders in their area, Brooks had splashed photos of convicted sex offenders across the *NotW*'s front page. This, an appalled Jay told Brooks, was bound to spark violent reprisals. Attacks on suspected sex offenders would be a "natural and foreseeable consequence of a sensationalised campaign". It was "obvious as a matter of common sense" that reprisals would follow. When Brooks insisted instead that she had not foreseen any such thing, Jay lectured her that it would be "patently obvious to anyone else", apart, presumably, from a bigoted tabloid newspaper editor, that publishing those names and photos was "inflammatory" with "the foreseeable consequence that there might be physical violence".

Jay concluded that it was inevitable, as "plain as a pikestaff", that violent repercussions would follow that front page. When Brooks continued to disagree with the exasperated lawyer, while conceding that there had been two reported incidents of reprisals, Lord Justice Leveson stepped in to back up his legal front man and suggest to Brooks that the *NotW* would not have published those pictures if she "had appreciated that the public might react in the way in which it did in the two incidents" — that is presumably, if she had shared the hindsight wisdom of Mr Jay.[3]

This telling exchange revealed that, in the eyes of our legal elite, it is "obvious", "natural" and "as plain as a pikestaff" that the millions of *News of the World* readers were really a lynch mob in waiting. All it needed was an "inflammatory" front page from their favourite Sunday paper to set light to the ignorant bigotry of this wooden-headed collective, and make them immediately abandon their Sunday roast to go and torch a few

suspected paedophiles. Of those two reported incidents, one—
an attack on the flat of a convicted sex offender and some
accompanying unrest on a Portsmouth housing estate—has
often been exaggerated, while the other—the daubing of
"Paedo" on the house of a paediatrician in South Wales, probably by local children—has been mythologized so thoroughly
that it still makes regular appearances in the national media as
an infamous riot by a "mob".[4] Generalising from these small
incidents, Lord Justice Leveson felt easily able to judge the
inevitable reaction of "the public"—that's you and me and the
people next door—to the *NotW* front page. This discussion
seemed to make the prejudices of the Inquiry "as plain as a
pikestaff", confirming that it was effectively orchestrating a
respectable riot against tabloid readers.

Nothing illustrated better how attacks on the popular media
reflect disdain for the populace than the public reactions to the
closure of the *News of the World* in July 2011. The *NotW* was
Britain's best-selling Sunday paper that still boasted a readership of millions. Whether its view of the world was to your taste
or not (and it was generally not to mine), it was a 168-year-old
institution that brought pleasure and entertainment to many
people. When Rupert Murdoch's News Corp panicked and
rushed to close the *NotW*, in response to the scandal about past
phone-hacking at the paper, the closure was celebrated in some
circles as if it were a victory in a war. Which perhaps it was,
really—the culture war to sanitise what the masses are allowed
to see and read.

Billionaire Conservative MP Zac Goldsmith spelt out the
celebratory view of the closure: "It has got to be a good day for
Britain. I think the *News of the World* as an organisation is toxic
on almost every level. I think the country after Sunday will be a
better place."[5] At what some might expect to be the other end of
the socio-political spectrum, Pulp singer and man of the "Common People" Jarvis Cocker pretended to use the last-ever
edition of the *News of the World* to wipe his behind on stage at a
Scottish festival, and told the crowd, "That's the only thing that
piece of shit has been good for in 168 years."[6]

How, exactly, would the end of the *News of the World* with the loss of hundreds of jobs, several years after phone-hacking ended, make Britain a "better place"? By preventing the millions getting their dose of "toxic… shit" on a Sunday, of course. Many others took a different view of the closure—half of *News of the World* readers were so disappointed they did not bother buying a different Sunday paper. Labour leader Ed Miliband announced that the closure had been a victory for "people power"; it looked more like a triumph for the twittering elite over the people they hold in contempt.

When, in February 2012, Murdoch announced the launch of the *Sun on Sunday*, there were cries of disgust from his influential critics—Labour MP Chris Bryant protested, "What creature will come forth from the swamp that we would want to see on our streets?"[7] Alongside this horror-fantasy vision of a newspaper that had not even been published, there were appalled warnings that the *Sun on Sunday* would merely be the *News of the World* in disguise. That did not deter the readers— the first edition sold more than three million copies, much to the disgust of the critics. Presumably those millions did not all buy it to use as loo paper. (However, they may have been disappointed to find that the *Sun on Sunday* turned out to be rather tamer and duller than its predecessor, under the cloud cast by the Leveson Inquiry.)

"Not Fit for Vulgar Persons"

From the first, history shows that the arguments about the media and press freedom in Britain have never been simply about standards and codes or the law. They have been about attitudes towards the people who consume the press and shape its preoccupations.

Broadly speaking, those who fear and loathe the mass of people and their passions have always favoured more controls over what can be published and distributed to them. Once that might have meant the king's censors trying to limit and license the printing press and punish those who printed outside their remit. Now it is more likely to mean the courts and media reform campaigners trying to impose "ethical" restraints and find some less brutal way of punishing those who stray.

On the other side, it would be a considerable stretch to claim that those who exploit the freedom to publish always have the highest interests of humanity at heart. The press barons pursue their own agendas and economic interests and often take a dim view of their readers' intelligence and appetites, subscribing to the old saw that "nobody ever lost money by underestimating public taste". (Which, incidentally, is not quite true—see the failure of the trashy *Sunday Sport* for a start.)

However, away from caricature press barons with pound signs for eyes, those who genuinely believe in an unfettered press have always based that belief on a faith in people's ability to hear and read everything and decide for themselves between right and wrong. Belief in press freedom is founded on a belief in the human capacity to choose. In this respect it is little wonder that support for a free press has tended to flourish at those moments and in those situations where popular movements for change are making progress and belief in the positive capacity of humanity is on the rise. There were sudden outbreaks of a flourishing press in England during the revolutionary era of the seventeenth century, in America during its own years of revolution a century later, and across Europe during the democratic upheavals of the 1800s. Many blogs and online publications have sprung up before more recent periods of protest in the Arab world and elsewhere.

At other times when misanthropy is on the march and faith in humanity is in decline—such as in Western culture today— then media-bashing comes more into fashion, as a proxy for expressing distaste for the people who have so disappointed their governments and society's elites.

Either way, history suggests that how you see the mass media and its problems broadly reflects what you think of the mass of people. This is not good news for the high-minded crusaders for more regulation of the press. It means that they are on the wrong side, not only of the historic struggle to win and defend freedom of expression, but also of the divide between humanist democrats and misanthropic miserabilists.

It is worth once more stepping out of the febrile atmosphere of today to try to put current issues in some brief historical perspective. It might remind us of how long and arduous has been the struggle for a free press on which it seems some would now so casually turn back the clock. It might also reveal how the current contempt for the "popular" press represents a recast version of some enduring elite fears about the masses and a mass media. Once, a King of England told parliament that freedom of speech was "not fit for vulgar persons" (meaning MPs); now our modern MPs are more likely to insist that they believe in a free press, "But..." vulgar papers are not fit for that freedom.

The "press" refers in the first instance to the printing press, introduced to England by William Caxton in 1476. It offered the opportunity to educate and inform the populace as never before. There followed more than 500 years (and counting) of conflict over how freely the press could be used and by whom. Throughout that time the issue has never been simply about what you think of words or books or newspapers (or, we can now add, websites), or about what is on page 3 or page 303. It has always fundamentally been about people, and what you think of humanity.

Five hundred years ago in the beginning of the press age, at the dawn of the modern era, the authorities were quite explicit: they were against the freedom to print because they were opposed to free-thinking in all its forms. They did not want even that small section of the population that could read to be able to question and discuss either religious or civil matters of importance. Issues of state were only for the King and his court to consider, just as the Bible was only to be read by priests (in Latin, not English).

The first measures to control the press were imposed in response to the first signs of dissenting thought spreading in Tudor England, as Reformation ideas from Europe began to question the orthodoxy of the ruling Roman Catholic Church.

To prevent the spread of such heretical Protestant notions in 1529 King Henry VIII (who ironically was soon to break with Rome and found the Church of England) passed laws to prohibit and control all publications, to be enforced by the Star Chamber, a secret court of privy councillors and judges. Anything to be printed now had to be pre-approved by the state before publication. John Frith, who sought to use the printing press to bring Reformation ideas to an English audience in their own language, was declared a heretic and ordered to be burned to death for his crimes.

Through the sixteenth and into the seventeenth centuries, Henry's daughters Queen "Bloody" Mary and Elizabeth I, and the Stuart kings James and Charles who followed them, passed harsher measures in a bid to control the press and prevent people reading unauthorised material. Nothing could legally be published unless it was licensed by the authorities and printed by the official Stationers' Company. Anything that criticised the King or his government could be branded as seditious libel. Not even Members of Parliament were deemed to have the right to freedom of expression. James I told them that "freedom of speech... are no Theames or subjects fit for vulgar persons or common meetings".[8] In the 1630s James's son, Charles I, gave the Archbishop of Canterbury and the Star Chamber carte blanche to crack down on unlicensed printers: all publications had to pass the censors, and were only supposed to be sold by authorised vendors. Those who defied these early crude attempts to "regulate" the press faced more than a slap on the wrist or a flea in the ear: an insolent author had his writing hand cut off at the wrist under Elizabeth, while a Puritan lawyer whose writing was less than complimentary about the wife of Charles I had his ears removed.

The demand for freedom of the press exploded as the power struggle between King Charles and parliament came to a head around the English Revolution of the 1640s. As part of the spreading mood of political unrest came "the revolt of the pamphleteers", who published their unlicensed writings demanding religious and civil liberty. John Lilburne of the radical Leveller movement called for a free press and an end to state licensing which was "expressly opposed and dangerous to the liberties of the people". Another Leveller, William Walwyn, ended his pamphlet on religious freedom and civil liberty expressing the revolutionary hope "That the Presse may be free for any man".[9]

Many pioneers of the popular struggle for a free press were striving in the first instance for the freedom to express their religious beliefs. That the demand for freedom began as a demand for religious freedom is worth recalling in a modern age when it always seems to be assumed that religion is a force for repression. They blended their Protestant or Puritan thought with the new rationalism of the coming Enlightenment, developing demands for civil and political freedom, too.

Even though it was often couched in religious terms, their argument for a free press was as much about Man as it was God. They believed that humanity had the God-given ability to understand, to reason, and to make the right decision about what was true. Therefore, there was no need for the authorities to protect people from any ideas by controlling the press. Man could consider all and judge for himself what was right. As the poet John Milton put it in his famous call for an end to licensing in *Areopagitica* (1644), "God gave him reason, he gave him freedom to choose, for reason is but choosing". Therefore man should have "the liberty to know, to argue, and to utter freely according to conscience, above all liberties".[10]

It is remarkable to contrast the view these seventeenth-century Puritans took of what Lilburne called "the meanest" in society with the current view of "ordinary people" among our enlightened cultural elite. They believed Man was a rational creature to be trusted with the freedom to say and read and think what his conscience dictated—not a fool in need of being protected or policed by his betters. Whatever we might think of their faith that God would ensure that truth would always out, their faith in humanity shines through the case for freedom of the press. (They still remained men of their times, of course—thus Milton was quite clear that his demand for a free press for all should not actually extend to the abominable Papists.) Today our liberal elite has largely lost faith in our humanity — and hence in freedom of the press.

In the tumult of the English Revolution in the 1640s the Star Chamber was abolished, the autocratic monarchy overthrown and the King beheaded. There was a brief flowering of a free press. Yet before long licensing of the press was back, first under Oliver Cromwell as Lord Protector and then under the restored monarchy of King Charles II. Charles appointed Roger L'Estrange as his official censor, with an army of spies to seek and destroy unlicensed writers and printers. L'Estrange made no bones about his opposition to the very idea of printing new-fangled newspapers for the masses, because "it makes the Multitude too Familiar with the Actions and Counsels of their Superiors... and gives them, not only an itch, but a kind of Colourable Right and License, to be meddling with the government".[11] He sought to contain the growing appetite for news and discourage "meddling with the government" by printing two official, government-approved papers. As late as 1663 a printer called John Twyn was hanged, drawn and quartered for infringing the Crown's monopoly on the licensed press and suggesting the king should be accountable to his subjects.

Yet the demands for freedom of the press grew alongside the popular movement for political reform. After the Glorious Revolution of 1688, when William of Orange and Queen Mary were shipped in to replace the autocratic James II, the press began to flourish. In 1694 Parliament, reluctantly in many cases, finally refused to renew the system of licensing and the Stationers' monopoly on printing ended. England and partic-ularly London entered the age of the newspaper (even though relatively few could read, so that many papers were read out loud in London coffee houses).

The end of licensing and outright bans did not mean the end of official attempts to keep the press away from the masses, however. Slightly more subtle measures were tried. In 1712 the government imposed the first stamp tax on paper, in a bid to make newspapers and other publications too expensive for the many. The threat of arrest and prosecution for seditious libel still hung over every writer and printer's head.

Yet the arguments for a freer press continued to grow in vigour and volume. From the 1720s, two English journalists writing under the pen name "Cato" began publishing essays in the *London Journal* arguing for freedom of the press as the means for a free people to know the truth and hold its rulers to account. There could be "no such thing as publick liberty without freedom of speech", argued Cato, and turned his fire on any government measures that would restrict it, such as stamp taxes and punitive libel laws.

Cato argued for freedom of the press in robust terms that seem far removed from the mealy mouth expressions of "support" that we hear for it three centuries later. Yes, he admitted, a free press would sometimes libel somebody. But, declared Cato, "I must own, that I would rather many libels should escape than the liberty of the press should be infringed".[12] It would be something of a surprise to hear the polite lobbyists for reform of the libel laws come up with any such unequivocal statement for press freedom today. These English essayists were to inspire the American Revolutionaries of the later eighteenth century who wrote the First Amendment to their United States Constitution, which states "Congress shall make no law abridging the freedom of speech, or of the press".

Yet as popular movements for political reform and democracy grew, the British elite became far more fearful of the spread of the press. The Wilkes riots of the 1760s, which were discussed in my first chapter, proved a turning point for some in their attitude to newspapers and the spread of "dangerous" information and ideas among more and more people. The frightening spectacle of huge crowds rioting in London in defence of liberty, and for the right to choose their MPs and to read newspaper reports of the proceedings of parliament, unnerved the authorities. As one MP said during the attempt to crack down on newspapers reporting what was said in parliament, "It is unfit that the people should be misled by printers and it is for their good that they should know nothing but came from the authority of this house".[13] The crowds rioting for "Wilkes and Liberty!" outside parliament made clear that they refused to accept "that they should know nothing", even if it was for "their [own] good".

Tax on Knowledge

If you can't ban them, tax them into oblivion. In the late eighteenth and early nineteenth century, seeing that it was no longer so easy to ban or license newspapers, the authorities sought to restrict the readership of the growing radical press, particularly among the new working classes. If they could not control all newspapers, they would strive to keep them out of the "wrong" hands. One way of doing this was to try to tax people out of the "market place of ideas".

By 1815 the stamp tax on newspapers had reached four old pence a copy, putting the press out of the price range of ordinary workers. Some radical publishers paid the stamp duty but branded it a "Tax on Knowledge" on their front page. Others simply ignored it and printed cheap, unstamped papers with titles such as *Black Dwarf*.

Matters came to a head after the infamous 1819 Peterloo Massacre in Manchester, when a mass rally for parliamentary reform in St Peter's Field—the booming industrial city still had no MPs to represent it at that time—was charged by the cavalry, leaving an estimated 15 dead and up to 500 injured. The government of Lord Castlereagh quickly moved, not to reform parliament, but to suppress the protest movement and the press that led it. Parliament passed the draconian Six Acts, two of which aimed to reduce and hopefully destroy the influence of the radical press among the people. It was clear that it was not merely the material published that so concerned the authorities, but the sort of people who might read or hear it.

One new law, the Blasphemous and Seditious Libels Act, toughened the punishments for publications judged guilty of these catch-all offences against the political and religious establishment. The maximum penalty for authors and editors of such articles was increased to 14 years transportation — that is, banishment from Britain.

The other new law dealing with the press, the Newspaper and Stamp Duties Act, widened the net of publications required to pay tax. The tax would now hit for the first time those which published opinion — political ideas — as well as those publishing news. Publishers also had to deposit a hefty bond of up to £300 with the authorities in advance of printing anything, as cover against future fines for seditious or blasphemous libel. The government made clear that the extension of the "Tax on Knowledge" was explicitly intended to curtail the availability and influence of pamphlets or newspapers that might "excite hatred and contempt of the Government and holy religion". One such newspaper was the *Manchester Observer*, which coined the title "Peterloo" (an ironic reference to the 1815 Battle of Waterloo), and was branded by a Home Office report as "the organ of the lower classes", which aimed to "inflame their minds". The *Manchester Observer* was eventually closed by the crippling costs of prosecutions under the new laws.[14]

Those who sought to defy these laws, so as to carry on exciting contempt of the government among the common people and inflaming the minds of the lower orders, faced harsh punishments. Prominent among the radicals who ignored the new law was Richard Carlile, who continued to publish *The Republican* from his shop in Fleet Street without paying stamp duty. Carlile was convicted of blasphemy and seditious libel, fined an eye-watering £1500 and sentenced to three years in jail. His wife Jane took over *The Republican*, for which Carlile continued to write from his prison cell. In 1821 Jane Carlile too got two years in jail for seditious libel. A few months later the next publisher of *The Republican*, Richard Carlile's sister Mary, had joined her in prison for the same offence.

While his family were adding to the prison population, Carlile campaigned from his cell for financial support for the paper, and for volunteers to defy the law by selling it. A rival paper, the *Morning Chronicle*, scoffed that "we can hardly conceive that mere attachment to any set of principles without any hope of gain or advantage will induce men (in any number) to expose themselves to imprisonment for three years". However, large numbers of men and women proved willing to do just that. More than 150 of them were sent to prison for selling *The Republican*. According to one account, "All told, they served over 200 years of imprisonment in the battle for press freedom".[15]

As the campaigns for parliamentary and other reforms grew in the 1830s, leading to the birth of the Chartist movement and spreading fear of another English revolution in government circles, more radical publishers faced fines and jail sentences for refusing to pay stamp duty on their newspapers. This did nothing to put off their readers. By 1836 it was estimated that the top six unstamped newspapers had a combined circulation of around 200,000, beating the sales of a pro-government stamped newspaper such as *The Times* many times over. That same year parliament bowed to the inevitable, accepted that it could not stem the tide of popular prints, and reduced the four pence stamp tax to one penny. It also lifted the tax on pamphlets. The tax on knowledge and newspapers was not finally abolished until 1855.

Fast forward exactly 300 years from the imposition of the first tax on newspapers in 1712. In January 2012 Jeremy Hunt, the Tory Secretary of State for culture and the media, tells a committee of MPs that the government favours giving the new post-Leveson regulator some "statutory underpinning", so that it has "proper sanction-making powers" to discipline the press, in the same way that the General Medical Council does with the medical profession. The Secretary of State suggested that only those publications which agreed to obey the new regulator and the new rules might be legally defined as newspapers and thus entitled to a zero rating for Value Added Tax (VAT).

Newspapers required by government legislation—sorry, "statutory underpinning"—to obey a body with "proper sanction-making powers", and those that object punished by being made to pay an extra indirect tax? That sounded something like a backdoor twenty-first century version of the old system of state licensing and taxing of the press. Perhaps more surprisingly, Hunt gave credit for the idea of slapping dissident newspapers with VAT—a stamp tax in all but name—to Alan Rusbridger, editor of the *Guardian*.[16]

But then, even when it was founded as the *Manchester Guardian* after Peterloo, that newspaper was viewed as a middle class outlet which paid the stamp duty and sniffed at popular papers that refused to. The working class *Manchester and Salford Advertiser* dubbed the *Guardian* "the foul prostitute and dirty parasite of the worst portion of the mill-owners".[17] What would they have said about it giving the Tories tips on how to tax papers that won't toe the line?

Intellectuals Against Newspapers

Ending the tax on newspapers did not abolish the prejudice against the popular press and its readers, which has continued to thrive in different forms to this day. As the twentieth century approached, and the British working classes became more organised and educated, the Victorian establishment became more contemptuous and fearful of their reading matter—and more so still after the emergence of fully industrialised printing and proper mass newspapers. When Lord Northcliffe launched the first of these, the *Daily Mail* in 1896, he declared that in order to maximise sales and profits it would "deal with what interests the mass of people". These words struck horror into the hearts of many others in the upper echelons of late Victorian Britain.

By now it had become tricky for the elites to condemn or attack "the mass of people" directly. The parliamentary reform acts of 1832, 1867 and 1884 had gradually extended the right to vote to more and more working men (women would be denied the vote into the twentieth century). The Education Act of 1870, which created the framework for the schooling of all children aged between 5 and 12, had helped to boost working class literacy. The organised trade union movement was becoming a power in the land. Away from the privacy of a gentleman's club, it was no longer so easy to get away with talking about the mass of the public as an ignorant mob or the scum of the earth.

In response the elite displays of contempt for the public went further underground. Instead of the upfront attacks of the past, they would express their fear and loathing of the people in code, often by focusing their assault on the newspapers and media consumed by the many. Laying into the vulgarity of the popular press became a proxy for thrashing the vulgar plebs who bought and read it. Mass newspapers were denounced as a cultural evil of the modern age for their "base content" — but their real crime was to be seen speaking to "what interests the mass of people".

The condemnation of newspapers was no longer confined to arrogant kings and their bullying ministers. In the late nineteenth century and the first half of the twentieth, the most vitriolic abuse aimed at the popular press came from the intellectuals and literati at the heights of cultural sophistication. These people often failed to hide their true feelings as others might, and made explicit that their loathing of newspapers was aimed at the readers.

Many eye-opening examples of this intelligentsia-against-newspapers tendency can be found in John Carey's brilliant *The Intellectuals and the Masses*. Carey has them all bang to rights, from the German philosopher Friedrich Nietzsche declaring that the rabble "vomit their bile, and call it a newspaper", to the English author D.H. Lawrence suggesting that schools should be closed and reading discouraged to protect workers from those "tissues of leprosy", popular books and newspapers.[18]

The writer H.G. Wells saw the mass press as dangerous because it pandered to people's base opinions: "A popular newspaper was, in a quite literal sense, a 'poison rag'." The author George Gissing believed that the new mass newspapers reflected "the extending and deepening Vulgarity" of the great mass of people, and were "the very voice of all that is worst in our civilisation". Carey observes that the character John Pether, a revolutionary agitator in Gissing's *Workers in the Dawn*, is obsessed with newspapers and burns to death when a pile of them catch alight on his bed: "The danger of inflammatory journalism could scarcely be more graphically illustrated."[19]

Even George Orwell, a radical journalist and author who remains the hero of many on the British Left, was not immune to the intellectual prejudice about the malign influence of the mass media on people. In Orwell's classic novel *1984*, Winston Smith observes that "If there is hope, it lies in the proles"—the working proletariat. Yet what hope could there really be for those whom Orwell depicts as brainwashed by the made-up news and entertainment—"Prolefeed"—that is pumped out from Big Brother's Ministry of Truth, including "rubbishy newspapers containing almost nothing except sport, crime and astrology"?[20]

On the other side of Europe's battle lines from Orwell, the young Adolf Hitler shared the European intellectual elite's disgust at the cultural degeneracy of the masses, a view forcefully expressed in *Mein Kampf*. "Like many English intellectuals, [Hitler] blamed this degeneracy on the mass media, deploring the poison spread among the masses by 'gutter journalism' and 'cinema bilge'."[21]

From the English literati to nascent Nazis, the elites of the first half of the twentieth century decried the mass media as a cipher for expressing their disgust at the masses: for popular press, read populace. Their real concern was not so much low press standards as the low culture of the lower classes who consumed it. Unlike H.G. Wells or Hitler, that view of the press is not dead and gone.

The Left's Law of Inverse Proportion

A supplementary question to the one that opened this chapter: how did "popular" become a dirty word even, or especially, among those who pride themselves on standing for "the People"?

In more recent times, there has been another twist on popular press-bashing. It is no longer kings and courtiers or Victorian authoritarians leading the assault on the mass media. The modern Left, in politics and academia, has been in the forefront of the culture war against the tabloids since the Second World War. One rule which has not really changed, however, is that what they say about the mass media reflects what they think about the masses.

As support for the Labour Party declined among working class voters over the past 60 years, the problem of the tabloid press rose up the party's agenda. There has been a sort of law of inverse proportion at work here: the less fulsome support Labour and the Left receive from voters, the more fierce their attacks on the mass media become; the less certain they are of the loyalty of working class people, the more certain they become that the popular press is exerting a malign influence. Labour has effectively projected its own bitter disappointment with the masses onto the mass media.

Hence Labour's attempts to tame and regulate the popular press reached a peak during the dark years of the Thatcherite 1980s, yet receded when Tony Blair's New Labour was in its electoral pomp and enjoying the media's blessing alongside electoral success. They burst forth once more in a feverish bout of tabloid-thumping and Murdochphobia as New Labour declined and fell at the 2010 general election.

Of course there is nothing wrong with Labour supporters attacking the Tory press, which often deserves all that it gets and more. However, the bitter complaints about mass media bias against the Labour Party, about the tabloid press dishonestly influencing elections, about Rupert Murdoch acting as "the puppet master" of British politics, all rest on an essentially low opinion of the electorate. The implicit message is not so very different from that eighteenth-century MP who wanted to restrict the reporting of parliament in order to prevent people being "misled by printers" and to protect them "for their good". The message today is that the public are not to be trusted with exposure to the manipulative mass media, that the mass of voters are either too gullible or apathetic to resist the influence of the tabloid ring-masters.

The tone of the Left's post-war argument about newspapers was set by the National Union of Journalists in its call for a Royal Commission on the Press in 1946. The NUJ conference complained that the growth of "commercial newspapers with millions of circulation has reduced news to the quality of entertainment". The link between mass readership and the lowering of standards, of newspapers having "reduced" the quality of news to pander to the millions, was as clear as any Tory snob could have made it.

As discussed earlier, the Left was also fearful that "the gramophone press" could make voters dance to their Tory tune at the 1945 general election. Even though Labour won its land-slide victory, it remained convinced that something must be done about the influence of the Tory press. This conviction grew stronger after the Conservatives returned to power through the 1950s, with the first serious loss of support for Labour among working class voters.

The Labour demand somehow to shackle or silence the tabloid press became more desperate in the 1980s, as Margaret Thatcher's Conservatives swept all before them. There was much talk of the death of Labour—and a conviction that the popular press had assisted in the killing. The Labour Left projected its own political crisis on to the mass media, seem-ingly convinced that its defeats were the fault of the Tory press, rather than having anything to do with the failure of Labourist politics.

As state-socialists who believed in control from above, many on the Labour Left had never been particularly devoted to a free press. In the crisis of the 1980s Labour enthusiastically embraced the idea of statutory backing for broader and stronger press regulation. Several Labour MPs brought forward their own parliamentary bills and initiatives to try to tighten regulation, seemingly in the belief that changing the press laws on paper could somehow alter political realities in the world outside parliament.

That these 1980s initiatives were really about Labour's declining political support rather than falling press standards is clear from the focus on establishing a legal right to reply. The question of whether those unfairly attacked in the press should have the right to publish a reply in the same newspaper has long been debated and remains an issue today. However, as with all questions ostensibly about press standards and ethics, it means different things at different times.

In the 1980s it was mainly about establishing the right of the trade unions and Labour to respond to attacks on them in the popular press. Obsessed with the hold that they imagined the tabloids had over malleable working class voters, Labour MPs and trade union leaders grasped at a legal right to reply as their only chance to break the spell. The dire consequences that giving such a legal right, in the words of the TUC, to anybody "who believes their views have been misrepresented by the media" might have for the future of a free press did not seem to matter.

This issue came to a head during the miners' strike of 1984–85, the peak of the eighties class war. The National Union of Mineworkers and its president, Arthur Scargill, were subjected to a stream of abuse and malicious allegations in the press. In response the unions representing print workers and journalists used their muscle in the industry to get statements in support of the striking miners' published in several national newspapers, exercising what some called "an industrial right to reply".

After the Thatcher government defeated the miners' strike, however, the power of the trade union movement was broken. In January 1986 Rupert Murdoch sacked his print workers and moved his whole operation to a new non-union plant at Wapping. The bitter struggle that followed ended the print unions' influence. As one sympathetic Left-wing account puts it, these setbacks for the unions "effectively removed the option of an industrial right to reply from the political agenda, and thereafter the pressure for change became centred more on parliamentary action".[22]

In other words: the worse the labour movement was defeated, the more it lost support and influence, the further Labour politicians retreated into seeking new laws to restrain the popular press that they blamed for their woes. The law of inverse proportions was in full working mode.

Radical academics and intellectuals also came to the fore in the 1980s and into the 1990s, championing various critiques of the mass media and its influence over the audience. Different schools of media studies and cultural studies developed competing theories and seemed to be constantly shifting their intellectual ground. Most basically began from an attempt to explain why the mass of working class people were not supporting Labour or the Left, even in times of economic hardship, without pinning the blame directly on the failure of Labourist politics. Their common response was to emphasise the cultural role of "ideology" as a force separate from economics, its powerful messages carried by the media. Opinions among the academic experts might differ as to how far the public was a passive recipient of these messages, or how far the audience could decode them for itself according to its location or identity in society. All, however, emphasised the centrality of the relationship between the media and the masses in shaping public consciousness in the age of "Thatcherism" and beyond. Stripped of their impenetrable academic language, these theories were effectively putting forward different intellectuals' versions of the "I blame the meejah" story—which had the added bonus of underlining the importance of media and cultural studies academics in countering its malign influence. The influence of these obscure theories has since spread some way beyond university seminars, to help shape public discussion of the problems of the press.[23]

The political attempt to rationalise the lack of support for the left as a product of tabloid press influence over the masses came to a head around the 1992 general election. With Thatcher gone and the grey Tory John Major presiding over an economic crisis, Neil Kinnock's Labour Party was convinced it would win. When instead Labour lost for the fourth successive election, and Rupert Murdoch's favourite paper foolishly boasted that "It's the *Sun* wot won it!", Labour had an anti-tabloid tantrum. Kinnock blamed the press for his defeat and threatened to go to the Press Complaints Commission, as if that body could somehow reverse the election result. Meanwhile, with Murdoch personally handing out a "huge bollocking" to the *Sun*'s editor for that headline, the paper changed its tune. It labelled Kinnock a "whinger" and said the notion that the press had duped the electorate was "an insult to the intelligence of the 14 million people who voted Conservative".[24] Indeed it was—as big an insult as the original headline had been. Both endorsed the view of the papers as Pavlovian masters making the mutt-like electorate dance.

Meanwhile, back in the real world, one other major event of the late 1980s demonstrated the limits of how far tabloid newspapers held their readers in thrall, if the critics had only cared to look. After the 1989 Hillsborough disaster, in which 96 Liverpool football fans were crushed to death, the *Sun* ran an infamous front page headlined "The Truth", which managed not to include one iota of that precious commodity. Acting on information from the police, the paper not only blamed drunken supporters for the tragedy, but also claimed that they had urinated on rescuers and robbed the dead. The backlash against these lies was swift and widespread. In Liverpool the *Sun* was publically burnt and permanently boycotted by thousands of erstwhile readers. The paper's sales on Merseyside have never recovered, despite numerous subsequent apologies. It was the *Sun* wot lost them, with a little help from its friends among police commanders and Tory politicians.

An Epidemic of Murdochphobia

After Tony Blair courted the support of the Murdoch press and New Labour romped to victory in the 1997 general election, the heat rather went out of the attacks on the tabloids. In that period public debate was more about the government allegedly "spinning" the media. Blair won three elections with the backing of the *Sun*. However, as his government sank deeper into crisis and unpopularity, Blair suddenly rediscovered Labour's criticism of the mass media's influence over politics. In what was billed as one of his last major speeches before being replaced by Gordon Brown as New Labour leader and prime minister, Blair turned on the media as a "feral beast" that "hunts in a pack" with a "seriously adverse" impact on "the way public life is conducted". He also generously admitted his own "complicity" in creating this state of affairs, and said New Labour had paid "inordinate attention" to "courting, assuaging, and persuading the media".[25]

The aftermath of New Labour's decline and fall, marked by the desertion of the Murdoch press from its camp and a crushing defeat at the 2010 general election, brought on a fresh, far wilder spasm of tabloid-bashing among Labour supporters displacing the blame for their crisis. As they sought an explanation that could get them off the hook, an epidemic of Murdoch-phobia swept Labour's ranks.

After Gordon Brown was ousted as prime minister in 2010, the former Labour leader all but disappeared from public life. The one speech he did turn up to make in the House of Commons was, to nobody's great surprise, a shrill rant accusing News International of having "descended from the gutter to the sewer" and being part of the "criminal-media nexus".[26] Did Brown raise these criminal allegations during his many apparently amicable meetings as prime minister with the Murdochs and their people? Or had his wife, Sarah, told Rupert Murdoch's daughter Elizabeth Freud and News International executive Rebekah Brooks that they were sewer rats when she invited them to a sleepover at the prime minister's country residence? It seems that only once New Labour had lost did the scales fall from their eyes and the realisation dawn as to who was really to blame for everything.

When Rupert Murdoch appeared before the Leveson Inquiry in April 2012, the house journal of the Labour Left branded him on its front page as "The puppet master", accused of manipulating our democracy.[27] Labour MP Tom Watson, a close aide of ousted prime minister Brown, went on a fantastic anti-Murdoch crusade on behalf of his fallen master. Murdoch and his media lieutenants, claimed bruiser Watson in his ridiculous book *Dial M for Murdoch*, were running a "shadow state". Murdoch not only exercised "a poisonous, secretive influence on public life" but actually "orchestrated public life from the shadows", with a "corrupt grip on our national institutions", manipulating "prime ministers, ministers, parliament, the police, the justice system" and spinning "an invisible web of connections and corruption".[28] The web might have been "invisible", but Watson and other Labour MPs could still somehow see it. What they could not see was that New Labour's defeat might have been due to the exposure of its exhaustion and political emptiness in the glare of public debate, rather more than any secretive influence exercised by the Murdoch press from the shadows.

It is of course true that Murdoch and his big media outlets have been influential, and that his British papers supported Thatcher and, more reluctantly, Major, before switching to New Labour in 1997 and then, even more reluctantly, back to Cameron's Conservatives in 2010. No doubt it is also true that reading Murdoch's *Sun* and *News of the World* (or other tabloids) was unlikely to have a radicalising effect on voters. Yet the notion that he has exerted an authoritarian "malign influence" over politics is just an easy way for Labour to explain away the profound changes in British political life and excuse its own loss of influence.

Labour's support among the manual working classes collapsed from 62 per cent in 1959 (and even then they lost the election) to just 38 per cent when Thatcher won her post-Falklands landslide in 1983. Are we meant to believe that Murdoch singlehandedly stole those millions of tabloid-reading voters out of Labour's pocket and delivered them to the Tories? The increasingly hysterical anti-Murdoch outbursts express the Left's refusal to face up to its own shortcomings, and its bitter view of the public as readily brainwashed saps who had let down the Labour Party, rather than the other way around. After all, puppet masters can only manipulate lumps of wood with no minds of their own.

I recall at the end of the 1990s, during a public debate about the future of the press, pointing out to the assembled left-liberal media people that if Rupert Murdoch did not exist, they would have to invent him, such was the role he played as a folk-devil symbol of all that was wrong with their world. By 2012 that irrational outlook had only intensified to the point where, as two journalism academics observe, for many of their colleagues almost every issue now features the appearance of "'Murdoch' as metaphor" for the ills of the media and society.[29]

The question of ownership of the press, and the concentration of media ownership in few hands, has long been a problem. But the radical tabloid-bashers (who generally give the Labour-supporting *Mirror* an easy ride) never want to address the other side of the issue: the failure to sustain public support for any sizeable alternative media. That is the problem with which anybody who wants to change the media needs to grapple—and without trying to blame the punters, many of whom rarely even read the popular press, for your inability to win them over.

History suggests that there is no reason to take at face value the high-minded posturing about press standards, media "puppet masters" and the need for greater regulation today. The underlying sentiment remains a disdain for the masses, and a wish to regulate or regiment the public by controlling the media that they are allowed to consume. The radical pro-regulation lobby today appears as keen to protect the public from itself as were the monarchists and authoritarians of yesteryear. It is a pity these modern-day radicals seem to lack the faith that the Puritans of yore displayed in the capacity of Man to read and judge everything for himself.

[1]   *Sky News*, 30 March 2012.
[2]   'Turn your back on page 3' campaign statement, 12 January 2012 (http://turnyourbackonpage3.wordpress.com/).
[3]   Rebekah Brooks at Leveson Inquiry, 11 May 2012 (http://www. levesoninquiry.org.uk/wp-content/uploads/2012/05/Transcript-of-Afternoon-Hearing-11-May-2012.pdf).
[4]   See Brendan O'Neill, 'A tale told too much—the paediatrician vigilantes', *Press Gazette*, 11 May 2012 (http://blogs.pressgazette.co.uk/wire/8897).
[5]   Quoted *BBC News Online*, 7 July 2011.
[6]   Cited in *Digital Spy*, 10 July 2011.
[7]   Labour MP Chris Bryant, letter to the *Evening Standard* (London), 20 February 2012.
[8]   David A. Copeland, *The Idea of a Free Press: the Enlightenment and its Unruly Legacy*, Medill School of Journalism 2006, p. 39.

9   *Ibid.*, p. 41.

10   *Ibid.*, p. 46

11   Cited in Andrew Marr, *My Trade: a short history of British journalism*, Pan Books 2004, p. 7.

12   *The Idea of a Free Press*, p. 99.

13   *Wilkes and Liberty*, p. 161.

14   See Stanley Harrison, *Poor Men's Guardians: survey of the democratic and working-class press*, Lawrence and Wishart 1974, p. 53.

15   *Spartacus Educational Website*, http://www.spartacus.schoolnet.co.uk/PRknowledge.htm

16   The *Guardian*, 16 January 2012.

17   *Manchester and Salford Advertiser*, 21 May 1836. Cited in Murray McDonald, 'Against the Guardian', http://neo-jacobins.blogspot.co.uk/2007/09/neo-jacobin-special-against-guardian.html

18   John Carey, *The Intellectuals Against the Masses: Pride and Prejudice among the Literary Intelligentsia, 1880–1939*, faber and faber 1992, pp. 7, 15.

19   *The Intellectuals Against the Masses*, pp. 121, 93, 105.

20   George Orwell, *1984*, Penguin 2008 edition, pp. 72, 320, 46.

21   *The Intellectuals Against the Masses*, p. 198.

22   *Regulating the Press*, p. 85.

23   For an academic critique of these trends see Andrew Calcutt and Philip Hammond, *Journalism Studies: a Critical Introduction*, Routledge 2011.

24   Cited in *BBC News Online*, 21 April 2005.

25   The *Guardian*, 12 June 2007.

26   *BBC News Online*, 14 July 2011.

27   *New Statesman*, 30 April 2012.

28   See Tom Watson and Martin Hickman, *Dial M for Murdoch: News Corporation and the corruption of Britain*, Allen Lane 2012, pp. 317, xvii, 1.

29   Andrew Calcutt and Mark Beachill, 'Murdoch as metaphor', Proof May 2012 (http://www.proof-reading.org/murdoch-as-metaphor).

Chapter Four

Why Blame "the Meejah"?

Who, we demanded to know in the summer of 2010, was responsible for the England football team's dismal display at the World Cup in South Africa? Was it our heroically abysmal players? The unintelligibly uninspiring Italian manager? The "sweet FA" blazers from the Football Association? Or, for those more patriotic souls, the optometrically challenged officials who failed to spot that Frank Lampard's "goal" against Germany had crossed the line almost as clearly as the Wehrmacht did in September 1939?

It was left to one of the UK's leading serious columnists, however, to cut to the heart of the matter. Despite not being, by her own admission, one of those "football aficionados", Polly Toynbee posed the big question. "Was it Rupert Murdoch", she demanded, "wot lost England the World Cup?"[1]

Never mind losing the World Cup; this sort of thing might make some wonder if perhaps the English intelligentsia had finally lost its marbles, due to the long-term effects of rampant tabloiditis and Murdochphobia. Such outbursts might even seem amusing, if they did not encapsulate a serious belief that the mass media is basically to blame for almost everything and must be given a kicking at every opportunity. Shooting the messenger has come to rival football as our national sport.

It seems that the media—especially the "popular" broadcast and print media and its proprietors—can be casually held responsible for just about any problem in society today. The

Murdoch press in particular has been accused of everything from corrupting British politics and policing to despoiling our culture, ruining our football and ravaging our women. Such is the one-eyed view of these matters that when the BBC announced compulsory redundancies in the summer of 2011, the outraged general secretary of the National Union of Journalists lost no time in blaming the public corporation's cuts on... Rupert Murdoch.[2]

If you think this is a cue for those satire websites to run a spoof news story about how Murdoch is even responsible for climate change—"The *Sun* blamed for global warming" (geddit?)—forget it. The humour-free zone of the serious press got there first. Typically *Rolling Stone* magazine's feature asking "Who's to Blame?" for "blocking progress on global warming" had the old stager Rupert Murdoch still sitting Madonna-like at Number One in its chart after all these years.[3]

The serious media also beat the satirists to the punch-line around the Leveson Inquiry. When *Private Eye* ran a spoof front-page report of the Inquiry as the "Salem Witch Trial" in which "A simple girl, Rebekah, confesses to being a disciple of the Devil, known to all as Murdoch, and begins to denounce the good folk of the town for consorting with the Evil One", it was only slightly sexing up the demonic depiction of Rupert Murdoch and Rebekah Brooks that had filled more serious reports of the proceedings—including some of those in *Private Eye*.[4]

And, though it sometimes seems that way, it's not just Murdoch. Whether the issue under discussion is childhood obesity or anorexia, gun crime or gay-bashing, war or recession, the plaintive cry of "I blame the meejah" has been heard across the UK and the rest of the West on countless occasions in recent times.

It seems remarkable that such an explanation of events should be so readily offered and accepted, yet be so shallow and deeply wrong. Those who quietly sneer at the intelligence of popular press readers should perhaps look to their own intell-

ectual laurels if they are prepared to subscribe to such an infantile conspiracy theory.

Nobody with a brain could claim that the media are unimp-
ortant in shaping events today. The giant modern media
machine of which the press forms part has unprecedented
influence and occupies a more central role in politics, culture
and everything else than ever before. And as we shall see in the
next section, nobody but a paid apologist could pretend that the
media and those who control it are innocent or have always
used their considerable influence for good.

Nevertheless, things are slightly more complicated than the
"blame the meejah" line might suggest. No newspaper or media
outlet is an island. They are connected to the rest of our culture,
both reflecting and reinforcing what is happening in wider
society. Despite all of the changes in its methods and its
standing, the "media" remains basically that: a collective med-
ium for transmitting messages and images; an agency for carrying information from one place to another.

The media reflects public life, and helps to shape our perceptions of it. So when you identify something wrong with
what's in the media, you are making a statement about what is
wrong with society itself. To blame the media for the state of the
world it shows us is akin to smashing the mirror because you
don't like the reflection you see. As a wise young German wrote
in a newspaper 170 years ago, the free press is as little responsible for the changing world that it reports on "as the astron-
omer's telescope is for the unceasing motion of the universe.
Evil astronomy!"[5]

The fashion for blaming the press for almost everything
brings to mind the surreal shoot-out in a carnival hall of mirrors
at the end of an Orson Welles movie, where the protagonists fire
at their multiple reflections rather than the real targets. The
media might not be innocent. But to find it guilty of causing
society's problems is to miss at least a large part of the point.
The old saying "Don't shoot the messenger" remains useful
advice.

Private Affairs

Is reality imitating the media, or vice versa? A look at problems for which the popular media is blamed today suggests that it is largely reflecting and transmitting cultural trends. These are cultural trends which emanate most powerfully not from the tabloid newsrooms but from the top of society's institutions downwards. If the media is guilty in these cases, it might appear more to be as an accomplice after the fact than as the prime suspect.

Probably the biggest allegation aimed at the popular press today is that they invade and "violate" people's privacy and turn personal matters into public property, without a reasonable excuse of acting in "the public interest". It is, in the words of one zealous campaigner "privacy-intrusion-for-profit" pretending to be news.[6]

Celebrities and public figures have filed into the UK courts to try to establish a legal right to privacy, asking judges to grant injunctions to prevent the press publishing information about them and to punish newspapers which have already done so. The issue of privacy became a hotter public issue around the phone-hacking scandal when it was revealed that a private detective hired by the *News of the World* had been trying to spy on "ordinary people" and high-profile crime victims as well as those who are willingly in the public eye.

For the chorus line of celebrities lining up to give evidence to the Leveson Inquiry into the British press in 2011–12, it seemed this cavalier attitude to privacy was a peculiar crime of tabloid journalism requiring special punitive measures.

Hugh Grant was as often the poster-boy and voice-over artist for the privacy police. The actor told Lord Justice Leveson that tabloid newspapers publish "almost no journalism now — it's mainly the appropriation, usually through illegal means, of British citizens' fundamental rights of privacy to sell them for profit". He supported more court injunctions to censor stories and demanded legally-backed sanctions to deal with "what I would call the privacy invasion industry; some people would call it the tabloid press".[7] Comedian and actor Steve Coogan attacked the tabloids as a criminal conspiracy or "protection racket". For him the idea of press freedom is a con-man's trick, "often used as a smokescreen to legitimise invasions of privacy". Coogan thinks that the injunctions and other court powers in place are not sufficient, and wants a privacy law to separate our old friend "genuine public interest journalism" from "tawdry muck-raking" by the tabloid press.[8]

Max Mosley, the former head of the Formula One motor racing industry, seemed more extreme in his personal predilections. He told Leveson that "invasion of privacy is worse than burglary" because you can replace stolen goods but "if somebody breaches your privacy, you can never repair the damage". Mosley wants a law that would stop the breach in the first place by enforcing "prior notification", where a newspaper has to warn you if it intends to publish a story. The subject could then go to an "enhanced regulatory body" with the power to stop the presses and prevent publication.[9]

Sounds as if the tabloids need a public dose of the sort of treatment Mr Mosley reportedly favours in private. They are singled out as a privacy-invasion industry, an illegal racket, that is breaching decent society's standards and must be subjected to special punishments.

But is press intrusion into the private arena really such an exceptional thing in today's society, so that it requires extraordinary measures and laws to deal with it? Or might it be viewed more as an extension of a general culture of voyeurism and exhibitionism where nobody seems too certain where the line between public and private ought to be any more? Are Leveson's lobbyists arrogant enough to assume that they can change the culture of the Anglo-American world by imposing a code or passing a law against it, as if they were so many celebrity Canutes?

The popular press hardly has a monopoly on violation of privacy. We live in an age where washing your dirty laundry in public, once deemed a cause for shame, has become a matter of pride—even a profession. There is now, after all, an entire class of celebrities who have achieved some fame and fortune by happily turning their lives inside out and peddling their private affairs for public consumption, via the media. The modern term "celebrity" was first defined half a century ago as one who is "known for his well-knownness" or as we might say now, famous for being famous.[10] Rather than achieving fame through public achievements, celebrities became famous simply for being seen in public, mostly thanks to the media.

Now things have gone a stage further. Members of the new class of celebrity that is all over the media today have become famous primarily through publicising their private lives and problems. That includes not only the likes of Jordan/Katie Price, her assorted husbands, and the cast of *The Only Way is Essex* or *Made in Chelsea*, but also more "elevated" figures such as Sally Bercow, the bedsheet-wearing wife of the speaker of the house of commons, and former Liberal Democrat MP Lembit Opik. While some worry about media intrusion, others clearly cannot wait to let the press and television into their intimate lives and will sell their privacy for a mess of potage, or its modern equivalent, 15 minutes of messy fame.

The "serious" celebrities who went to the Leveson Inquiry and parliamentary committees, dressed and talking like lawyers to call for action against press intrusion, insist that they are not like that, and do not invite publicity for their personal affairs. Yet one ironic and entirely uninvited upshot of the celebrity circus was that, as they trailed around the various legal inquiries and committees in 2011 repeating their tales of exactly how their privacy had been violated, many of us learned far more about the private details of Grant's love-child, Coogan's extra-marital affairs and Mosley's sado-masochistic pastimes than we would ever have hoped to hear. They too, it seemed, were willing to expose their privacy—in the "public interest", of course.

That is not the biggest inconsistency on the privacy issue. The stranger thing is that the hullabaloo about the invasion of privacy by tabloid papers is often led by the sort of politicians, public figures and media outlets that have themselves seemed keen to see more intervention in the private sphere—by the authorities. They don't want the tabloids invading the privacy of the "ordinary people" on whose behalf they claim to speak. Yet they have often backed state agencies and others intervening in people's family lives and personal affairs. Invading the privacy of some turns out to be OK if it is done for the "right" reasons by the right people or powerful institutions.

This double standard was highlighted, albeit unintentionally, by the villain of the Leveson Inquiry: former *News of the World* hack Paul McMullan, he of the "feral persona" who became infamous during his evidence as the only person to try to defend the decision to hack the phone messages of abducted schoolgirl Milly Dowler. McMullan went further still in spelling out his complete lack of sympathy for the defence of privacy. "In 21 years of invading people's privacy", he told Lord Justice Leveson, "I've never actually come across anyone who's been doing any good. Privacy is the space bad people need to do bad things. Privacy is for paedos. Fundamentally, nobody else needs it."[11]

Privacy is for paedos! This suggestion caused outrage in the serious media, the blogosphere and on planet Twitter. How dare the "evil", "rat-like" McMullan suggest that individuals and families who want some privacy from tabloid intrusion are up to no good! The consensus seemed to be that, to coin a tabloid phrase, hangin's too good for him.

However, the uncouth tabloid hack with his shabby outfit and opinions was only saying bluntly what many more cultured folk have effectively been arguing for years. Allegedly liberal middle class writers and campaigners have consistently argued the need for more intervention in family life by the authorities, in order to deal with the "dark side" of what goes on "behind closed doors". They are at least as suspicious of what "ordinary people" are up to as any "feral" hack.

The radical feminist lobby, for example, who would not be seen dead in the company of a creature such as Paul McMullan, have long insisted that the privacy of family life is a cover for sexual abuse and violence against women and children. As a leading encyclopaedia of philosophy summarises the feminist critique of privacy, "If distinguishing public and private realms leaves the private domain free from any scrutiny, then these feminists such as Catherine McKinnon (1989) are correct that privacy can be dangerous for women when it is used to cover up repression and physical harm to them by perpetrating the subjection of women in the domestic sphere and encouraging non-intervention by the state".[12] In other words, as the strictly non-feminist Mr McMullan had it, "privacy is the space where bad people do bad things".

In Britain, the National Society for the Prevention of Cruelty to Children is widely portrayed as the unimpeachable moral champion of the innocent. Yet NSPCC propaganda which points the finger of guilt at all parents and adults might also be thought to chime with the non-innocent McMullan's line. In recent years the NSPCC has run campaigns with cute slogans such as "Stop parents getting away with murder", and issued mass publicity warning that abusers are often those whom children trust the most. They call on neighbours, school dinner ladies and everybody else to keep an eye on what is going on behind somebody else's closed doors, because "it is likely that each of us will either know a child we suspect is being abused or know someone who does". Of course, we are supposed to understand that such high-minded charitable encouragement of public mistrust and mass snooping into other people's private sphere, in search of child abuse that might be hidden behind closed doors, is in no way to be confused with the notion that "privacy is for paedos".[13]

Even with the outrage against phone-hacking and tabloid intrusion in full cry, it seems that much of the liberal media had not woken up to the possibility of a contradiction in its attitude to privacy, which says it is not OK for a journalist to pry into a mailbox or a rubbish bag but it is, for example, somehow laudable for Jamie Oliver's army to poke their noses into our kids' school lunchboxes. Amid all of its endless reports of the Leveson Inquiry and the police investigation into tabloid intrusion in 2012, liberal newspapers found space to run various columns arguing that "we should be less squeamish about inter-

vening in 'chaotic' families", or that the government must intervene to help the many children being "trashed by families and
disregarded by the state", or that something must be done
about "the dangerous privacy of the home".[14]

It seems clear that the tabloid press are far from the only
ones with a fairly cavalier attitude to other people's privacy, or
who believe that essentially privacy "is for paedos" and bad
parents. If you want to see a powerful "privacy invasion
industry" in action, you might look to the parenting industry or
the welfare state—which has rather more power to affect
people's lives than the press.

So what are the media-bashers saying here? That invasion of
privacy by the popular press is to be condemned, but invasion
of privacy by the authorities, experts and do-gooding celebrities
is to be encouraged? Media intrusion bad, state intrusion good?
And is privacy to be seen once more as a privilege rather than a
right? Despite all the talk of protecting "ordinary people" there
seems to be a privacy hierarchy emerging, where the privacy of
delicate celebrities is deemed sacrosanct whilst that of rougher
"chaotic" families and people who don't even eat organic prod-
uce, never mind name their offspring after it, is seen as rather
more negotiable. So it is a terrible violation for an actress such as
Sienna Miller to be confronted by photographers as she goes
about her business, but apparently not so bad for a young teach-
ing assistant to be subjected to a compulsory Criminal Records
Bureau check to see if she is a sex offender before she is allowed
to take up a job. We are in a confused state of public and private
affairs.

Some might offer the counter-argument that, unlike the
authorities, the tabloids target innocent people who have done
nothing wrong. Leave aside for now the millions of innocent
people who have to be checked out as potential paedophiles
before being allowed to work, or even to arrange flowers in a
church, anywhere near a child. Try telling that to those who
have been officially but falsely accused of abuse and had their
children taken into custody, starting with the victims of the
Cleveland and "satanic abuse" panics of the 1980s and early

1990s—moral panics against working class families that have often been orchestrated and cheered on by the same sort of players in government and the media who are now behind the anti-tabloid crusade over privacy.

One of the highest profile victims at the Leveson Inquiry was Christopher Jefferies. He was the Bristol landlord of Joanna Yeates, a young woman murdered just before Christmas in 2010. When he was initially arrested by the police as a suspect in her murder, the tabloids went to town on Jefferies, probing into his private life and spraying around allegations and innuendo to present him, he later said, as a "dark, macabre, sinister villain... a lewd figure... a peeping Tom".[15] Jefferies was soon cleared of any involvement in Ms Yeates' murder, sued the papers concerned and won apologies and damages. He appeared before Leveson and was treated with universal sympathy by the Inquiry and the media. Who could imagine anything worse than being falsely arrested and linked with murder and other dark deeds in the press, by papers that appeared to think they could get away with anything in the name of pervert-hunting?

Well... how about being falsely accused of murdering your own child in the courts—and having your newborn baby impounded by the council? A three-year ordeal conducted, not in the mass media, but by the state in total secrecy. That was what happened to a young couple from London, Rohan Wray and Chana al-Alas, whose four-month-old baby died of a fractured skull in 2009. They were charged with murder and causing or allowing the death of a child, and their second child was taken away by the authorities at birth in 2010. They were eventually cleared of all charges at the Old Bailey after it was discovered that the baby had been suffering from severe rickets, which could have led to the fractures. Yet far from receiving any apology or damages, they then had to endure a second legal ordeal as Islington council went to the secretive family courts and again accused them of being responsible for their baby's death, in a bid to prevent the couple regaining custody of their toddler. Only when that allegation was also thrown out in April

2012, and the couple were finally reunited with the 18-month-old daughter they had not seen since her birth, was the media even allowed to report on this disgraceful case of "privacy intrusion" by a state which assumes it can get away with anything, in secret, hiding behind the banner of child protection.[16]

Now where could those wicked tabloids have got the idea from that it was OK to invade people's privacy and mess up their lives in pursuit of a righteous end?

From Journalism to Voyeurism

The popular media has indeed become increasingly pre-occupied with reporting on private affairs and scandals rather than public matters. The question is, why? There has always been a strong element of "human interest stories" since the birth of the mass press in the late nineteenth century. More recently, however, the trend has slipped from journalism to voyeurism, as captured in the outrageous treatment of Milly Dowler or the parents of Madeleine McCann.

The final edition of the *News of the World* was instructive in the changing character of tabloid news coverage down the years. Having launched in 1843 with the slogan "All Human Life Is Here", the *NotW* was never shy of exposing scandalous behaviour and publishing the gory details of sexual and violent crimes. However, once upon a time it did this more in the context of covering the great news stories of the day.

That final edition, published in July 2011, included a selection of front pages from the Sunday newspaper's history. The early ones chosen focused on the Titantic, two World Wars, the abdication crisis of 1936 or the Queen's accession to the throne in 1952 (alongside the odd infamous murder case). A noticeable change of tone and focus came in the covers from the sixties, with the June 1963 front page "Confessions of Christine — by the girl who is rocking the government", revealing the story of the call girl Christine Keeler whose affair with cabinet minister John Profumo helped to bring down the Tories.

The Profumo affair of course was a major political scandal splashed by the *News of the World*. The front pages which the final *NotW* reproduced from the past 30 years more often exposed the sex, drugs and other sordid personal scandals of royals, footballers and assorted celebrities (including, no doubt coincidentally, Hugh Grant), alongside the paper's crusade to expose child sex offenders and reports of the deaths of Princess Diana and the Queen Mother. It also included a couple of the *NotW*'s stand-out investigative exclusives—the 1999 revelation that Lord Archer had committed perjury in a libel case against the press, and the Pakistani cricketers' spot-fixing scandal of 2010. But the general drift seemed clear enough: away from the public towards the personal, and into the sort of ruthless gossip-hunting highlighted at the Leveson Inquiry that was eventually to lead the paper onto the rocks.

This quick survey of the *News of the World*'s drift towards voyeurism begs the question: why did it happen? It would seem ridiculous to suggest that the *News of the World*'s journalists and editors just became more puerile down the decades. It was not exactly edited by teenagers at the end, after all. The more sensible explanation is surely that these developments reflected a shifting sensibility in society. The *News of the World* changed as the world did, reflecting the way in which our society's sense of the line between what is considered private and what is in the public sphere has become as blurred and as uncertain as the moral compass of a bed-hopping celebrity.

It is not only tabloid hacks and downmarket reality TV producers who seem unsure where that line might be today. "Quality" television channels also turn out makeover shows where people are stripped bare physically and emotionally for public delectation, volunteering to have a motley selection of lifestylists, fashionistas, health fanatics, sex counsellors, obsessive cleaners and other alleged experts tell them what dull, filthy, fat, frumpy and frigid creatures they are. Everything from childbirth to death from cancer has now been deemed a suitable subject for full-colour close-up treatment by television.

Fewer people than ever before seem immune to the temptation to let it all hang out in public. When David Blunkett was Labour home secretary in 2004, he became embroiled in a paternity suit with a married publisher with whom he had an affair and a child. Both sides of that most personal of disputes conducted the argument in the media spotlight, briefing papers through leaks and "close friends", competing for public sympathy by exposing their family lives to the inquisitive media, and generally behaving more like the tell-all celebrity Kerry Katona than an august cabinet minister. Since then the spread of Facebook and Twitter have made it easier for many more to reveal their intimate lives and feelings to countless "friends" and followers. People will now tweet freely about everything from their bitter divorce to their grief over a bereavement, without any encouragement or payment from the press.

When everybody from a tabloid hack to a home secretary can seem equally blasé about the question of privacy, it should be clear that there has been a major shift in the cultural terrain. That shift has occurred under the watchful eye of the state.

At the same time as condemning and moving against privacy intrusion by the press, the UK state in the form of the government and the courts has itself become more closely involved in the private sphere. Much political action is now aimed at changing the way people behave and live their lives from the kitchen to the bedroom. Under New Labour this was described as "the new politics of behaviour". Under the Conservative-Liberal Democrat coalition, it became part of the "nudge" agenda. Whatever they call it, government action today is about trying to change the way we live at home and in private as well as in public, whether through campaigns against smoking, drinking and "unhealthy" eating, or the multiple new forms of official intervention in parenting and child-raising.

The state has also assumed new powers to check on what we might once have imagined were our private communications. The Regulation of Investigatory Powers (RIP) Act 2000 has been applauded by many when deployed against journalists and editors for phone-hacking. It should not be forgotten, however, that the purpose of the RIP Act was not primarily to criminalise snooping by reporters, but to legalise the many ways in which the security services and other state agencies are allowed to spy on the public with impunity.

Whenever questions are raised about the implications of state surveillance for privacy, the stock response of the UK authorities over the past decade has been to repeat the authoritarian cliché that "If you have nothing to hide, you have nothing to fear". Or to put it another way, privacy—which they call secrecy—"is the space that bad people need to do bad things". Unless you are a bad person, who needs privacy from the security state's prying eye?

In countless ways, what might once have been thought of as personal affairs have become the business of politics. Politicians now stand for election less on any public political principles than on their "personality" and "character". The allegation of sleaze bandied about at every election since 1997 epitomises this. The biggest political scandal of recent times—exposed via the media—was the furore over MPs' expenses claims, and provided great fun for all. But what was it really about? The MPs were being attacked over their personal probity and duck ponds rather than their political values or proposals for sailing HMS UK on wider seas.

The confusion of the public and the personal has reached the point where the supposed left-right battle between "Red" Ken Livingstone and "Bullingdon" Boris Johnson in the 2012 London mayoral election came down to a battle of the tax returns rather than the manifestos. The old political line, "The Personal is Political", began life as a 1970s feminist slogan demanding that personal issues of gender relations be elevated into political ones. Now things have gone way beyond that, so that big political debates have been reduced to the level of personal spats and gossip.

Or look at the Leveson Inquiry itself. Throughout its proceedings Lord Justice Leveson, his legal counsel Robert Jay and their supporting chorus of celebrities, police chiefs, politicians and respectable media figures were constantly sniffing about the intrusion of the popular press into people's private business in pursuit of "salacious gossip". Yet on occasions the

Inquiry seemed as obsessed with the minutiae of people's personal relations and communications as any tittle-tattle merchant. Some might claim that the big fuss made about the revelation that David Cameron texted "LOL" to Rebekah Brooks, and thought it meant Lots of Love, reflected the political importance of their relationship. Others might think Leveson, Jay and co were simply indulging in personal gossip for the media classes, something for the supper party tendency to LOL about.

We are a long way from the Greek philosopher Aristotle's clear distinction between the public and private spheres, where the family is discrete and the polis or public sphere is where important affairs are played out. The newspaper stories, TV programmes and celebrity show-and-tells all feed off this anti-privacy culture that has come from the top of society down.

"They **** You Up, Your Mum and Dad"?

There is a cultural shift at work here that cannot be put down to the popular press alone. They are simply taking advantage of the confusion over the private and public line to push the boundaries further—and sometimes considerably too far. Who stole our privacy if it was not just the tabloids wot done it?

Two trends at work since the 1960s might help to make sense of it. The first, amid the changes of the sixties, was the gradual loss of cultural authority of traditional morality and institutions, notably the family and family values. This counter-cultural revolt created a reaction against the notion of a closed-off private sphere—and not only among the hippies in communes who took the doors off their toilets. There was a healthy questioning of the old stiff ways of family life, particularly as they defined the role of women. That spun out of control into notions that the private sphere and family life were inherently suspect.

The slogan of the age became, in the words of Philip Larkin's 1971 poem *This Be The Verse*, "They fuck you up, your mum and dad/They may not mean to but they do". In the decades that followed, the sixties radicalism faded but the counter-cultural reaction against the private sphere became the dominant culture. By 2009 a top judge, Lord Justice Wall, raised in the sixties, even felt able to quote those profane Larkin lines from the bench while giving judgement in a child custody case between two divorcing parents.[17]

Turns out that it was not reactionary tabloids who invented the undermining of privacy. It was more of a misguided side effect of the radical upheaval of the sixties. What a shocker, as the papers might say.

This cultural questioning of the private sphere has been reinforced by another, more political trend, that took off in the sixties and has gathered force ever since. This is the trend for state agencies to view the family and the private sphere as an appropriate site for social policy interventions. The old notion of the home being somebody's castle, not to be invaded lightly by the authorities, has been replaced by the idea that the welfare state has not only a right but a duty to intervene to "support" those who are "vulnerable". These days "vulnerable" can mean just about everybody once the favoured categories of women, children, the elderly, the ill (mentally as well as physically), the socially excluded, disabled and anybody else deemed "at risk" has been added to the body count.

The motor behind this shift was not a sudden upsurge of social problems, but rather a downgrading of what was seen as the business of government and the state. Once, governments of every political stripe had declared their intention to pursue policies designed to create the Good Society. Now they appear to have given up on that noble goal, and reduced their aims instead to creating the Good Citizen (or Subject in Her Majesty's realm) by instructing us in how to live even behind our own front door.

Social problems have been reinvented as personal matters, but ones which must be subject to the caring intervention of the welfare state. When the authorities feel free to tell people what to feed their children or how much wine to drink at home, and families can be denied the right to adopt a child because an adult chooses to smoke (even in the garden), or patients denied health treatment because of what they eat, the writing is on the wall (though they will probably tell you to wash it off, unless it's state-sponsored graffiti art). There is no longer any consensus as to where the public starts and the private ends, or where state intervention should end and personal autonomy begin.

Little wonder against this confused and dehumanising background that the media should have picked up the anti-privacy baton and run with it further and faster than anybody else. That does not make it right. The unbridled invasion of privacy is bad news both for the press and its subjects. It does, however, make something of a nonsense of attempts to focus on the "privacy intrusion industry" of the tabloid press as the source of the problem.

Picking on too narrow a target in this way also leads the privacy campaigners to demanding too narrow, technical solutions — such as the idea that privacy laws or judges' injunctions can sort matters out. In facing up to the blurred line between the public and the private, we are dealing with the loss of a cultural anchor that has contributed to reshaping almost everything about the society in which we live. The notion that such a cultural shift can be reversed again by passing a law, issuing a judgement or imposing a code is absurd. It demonstrates the public arrogance of the judges and lawyers and their celebrity advocates that they should imagine they can turn the tide and alter the world and the way people live, simply by a wave of the judicial arm or a nod of the bewigged head on the bench.

Defending Privacy — and Press Freedom

This is not to decry the importance of defending the private sphere against all-comers. As it happens I believe as much as any of them that the defence of privacy is important. We all need a private sphere where we can withdraw to recharge batteries and prepare for another sortie into the world, somewhere we can think and talk and relate to one another away from interrogation or surveillance. In response to that government slogan, I confess that I certainly do have "something to hide" from public gaze. It is called my personal life and private business.

A proper private sphere is also the flipside of a properly developed public sphere, where we can conduct our society's collective affairs. Both will thrive only by being given some separate space. However, more laws and regulations to restrict the press in the name of privacy are not the solution. Indeed such measures can only make matters worse, by further encroaching on the conduct of public affairs. Thus France has the strictest privacy laws, which have often been used to shield the powerful from public examination as effectively as England's libel laws do over here.

A glance at history shows that there is no necessary contradiction between fighting for a properly free press and defending the cultural ideal of an inviolable private sphere. Many of those who led the struggle for press freedom in England in the seventeenth and eighteenth centuries also fought for the right to a secure private life, for every Englishman's home to be his private "castle" (and not only those who actually lived in castles). Thus John Wilkes' fiercest complaint against the government of his day was not only that they had arrested him for publishing criticisms of them, but that in the process his house had been violated and his personal papers impounded. In revolutionary America too, while the First Amendment to the Constitution insisted upon the inviolable freedom of speech and the press, the Fourth Amendment endorsed "The right of the people to be secure in their persons, houses, papers and effects, against unreasonable searches and seizures".

What united their desire for a free press and their desire for a private life was their deep suspicion of the state, and hostility to state interference in the public or private affairs of the citizenry. By contrast, what seems to unite today's wish to constrain a free press with the endorsement of official intervention into the private sphere is a deep suspicion of the populace, and a belief that the state must be called upon to save us from the media and, ultimately, ourselves. The state, whether in the form of Lord Justice Leveson or the secret family courts, is to be entrusted with everything from policing the press in public to intervening in people's private lives. That is a recipe for disaster in both spheres.

State intrusion is the central barrier to the clear delineation of the public and the private. More state intervention cannot be the solution. Take off the narrow anti-tabloid blinkers and it becomes possible to see that in assuming a cavalier attitude to privacy, the popular media is carrying a mainstream cultural message, not ploughing some maverick furrow. It will take another major cultural shift, a revolution in attitudes, to alter things once more and establish properly discrete public and private spheres. That will require the fullest possible public debate, not yet more restrictions on what can be reported or talked about in the first place.

A more intimate look, then, at the issue of privacy and intrusion suggests that the press and the popular media have become the scene for playing out a bigger game, reflecting and reinforcing wider cultural trends, rather than running amuck alone. That pattern appears true of other areas, too.

For example, many of us have been highly critical of the media for the way in which it tends to swamp public affairs with sentimentality, emotionalism and tears. The coverage of the death and funeral of Diana, princess of Wales, is often seen as setting the template for this trend. Yet it was prime minister Tony Blair, not the tabloids, who set the tone for the whole week-long national grief-fest by coining the name "the People's Princess". Nor did the media have to instruct statesmen and politicians such as Blair, Bill Clinton or more recently Ken Livingstone in the new art of how to cry for the cameras. Public figures on all sides who appear incapable of offering political leadership have proved keen to make a sentimental connection with the public by associating themselves with emotive causes and sympathetic victims via the media.

The mass media also comes in for justified criticism these days for scaremongering and encouraging exaggerated public fears about everything from avian flu to Islamic terrorism. Yet scratch the surface of these stories and you will generally find that the media is only really acting as a loudhailer for messages that emanate from state or quasi-state institutions, all of which now subscribe to the stultifying safety-first dogma of the "precautionary principle" and appear afraid of their own shadows.

Unnecessary food scares have often carried the official stamp of the Food Standards Agency; the wild suggestion that an outbreak of avian flu might necessitate the digging of "plague-style mass graves" to hold the thousands of dead came from the UK government's chief medical officer at the time; and it was the New Labour government which stoked unease by making plans to flee London in the face of a hypothetical terrorist "dirty" bomb — something Churchill ruled out even if the real Nazis were marching up Whitehall. More recently it was insecurity within the Tory-Lib Dem government, rather than among tabloid editors or motorists, that led ministers to call for the panic buying and stockpiling of fuel during the non-existent fuel shortage of March 2012. The politics of fear and panic that begins in these high places can certainly be spread epidemic-style by the media. But the papers and news channels are usually more the carriers than the source of the infection.

No doubt some official bodies will say that it is only by pitching their warnings and advice in a slightly sensational style that they can make the impact in the media they need to get their message across. This in turn raises a key question about the blame-the-media culture.

How have the popular press and the mass media come to matter so much to everybody in public life? Why is it that all of these cultural trends, from social voyeurism to moral panics, are now played out in the media first and foremost, so that every event and debate has to be in the papers and on TV or nowhere at all?

Less Popular Yet More Powerful?

To update the old philosophical question about a tree falling soundlessly if nobody is there to hear it: if an event is not in the media, did it really happen? The answer these days is apparently no, at least in the world of politics and public affairs.

A PR stunt by a handful of eco-protestors can become a national Event because it gets plenty of sympathetic coverage. On the other hand, an angry demonstration in central London by around 150,000 Tamils in April 2009 went almost unnoticed by everybody, because few in the media were interested in the war in Sri Lanka.

The UK press has become part of a wider media, concentrated in big conglomerates, that seems to bestride every aspect of British political life. The mass media was once a discrete but important element in a public domain where different institutions and interests vied for influence, from political parties and trade unions to churches and communities. Now the media seems to be the only real player on the pitch, the power to which all must come as supplicants, a dominant force that squeezes out every other aspect of political affairs.

No longer is the media an adjunct of Westminster politics — today things can appear to be the other way around. Careerist politicians might now prize a media image or an appearance on a TV panel show above a substantial speech in parliament. After all, in their square-eyed media-centric worldview the news is that looking like a chump on *Have I Got News For You* can get you elected mayor of London.·

How have we arrived at this point? The apparent dominance of the media over public debate and political affairs strengthens the notion that the all-powerful press barons and media moguls are controlling events — even running a "shadow state" as deluded critics describe the Murdoch media empire. Yet stand back for a moment. Is it really possible for the mass media to be more powerful than ever, at a time when it arguably has less of a connection with public opinion and sentiment than in recent memory?

Newspapers, as everybody knows, are in a parlous financial state after losing millions of readers collectively from their postwar peak years. Television channels too can now count on millions fewer viewers for most of their major programmes — particularly news and current affairs.

So how can the mass media simultaneously be less popular and yet more powerful?

The answer lies less in any increasing "power of the press" than in the deepening impotence of society's other institutions. The media has assumed its position of unprecedented influence by default. Whether we are talking about the Church of England or the Conservative Party, every other public body has withered over recent decades in terms of its authority and support. The media has become more or less the last man standing among the pillars of traditional authority.

This is how a press which reflects reality has also assumed such a major role in shaping it. Take the plight of the mainstream political parties, which are now empty shells of their former selves. Having misplaced millions of members and lost their roots in solid constituencies in society, how are Labour or the Tories supposed to relate to an audience or fight an election campaign? Only, as they see it, through the media. Thus British elections have become media affairs, conducted far less on the streets and doorsteps than on television screens, in newspapers and online.

These election campaigns look increasingly like what Daniel Boorstin—the man who defined celebrity—called "pseudo-events": staged and scripted affairs that truly would not happen if the media was not there to cover them. As a result the political agenda is often set not by contesting principles and heartfelt policies, but rather by what politicians imagine the media wants to see, and how best they think a message might "play" in the press or on TV. The impression given is that our leaders are dancing to Big Media's tune. But really these isolated wannabe statesmen are just desperately trying to catch the public's eye and can see no other stage on which to perform, like X Factor hopefuls dreaming alone in their bedrooms who believe that Simon Cowell holds their one ticket to stardom.

Speaking of Mr Cowell: one often-misunderstood example of how the media and politics work today can be seen in the omnipresence of celebrity culture. The mass media—and by implication its audience—is accused of dumbing down public affairs and trivialising the news by packing it with all manner of celebrity ephemera, gossip and fluff. Yet the political class itself has been as keen as anybody to promote the role of celebrity in public life.

Politicians bereft of public appeal or real popularity often try to hitch a ride on the designer coat-tails of media-friendly celebrities. That is why movie actresses and pop stars can turn up as special UN ambassadors and international peace envoys, or a TV chef can be adopted as an official crusader against junk food—a "national hero" as the Conservative Party conference voted to anoint Jamie Oliver in 2006. It is why a serious committee of serious MPs could, in April 2012, seriously invite the comedian Russell Brand to give them advice on combating drug abuse. It is also why those campaigning for reform of the UK press are happy to hide behind the Hollywood image of tabloid-bashing actors and celebrities they might otherwise disdain. The result of this process is that the news media is swamped by celebrity culture. The underlying cause of it, however, is the shrivelling of politics that has created a situation where it can appear that celebrities rule the earth.

The role of the media has expanded to fill the gap left by the decay of our broader public and political life. Its growing influence is a product of the withering of all that was once around it. Where once there were other voices and sources of information in the public arena, from political parties and churches to trade unions and organised communities, now there is only the multi-armed media. It is ironic to hear political veterans blame the cut-down media coverage of parliamentary debates for the lowering of their esteem in the public eye. In reality things happened the other way round: it was the declining authority and importance attached to what goes on at Westminster, among voters and MPs alike, that prompted papers such as *The Times* to abandon their tradition of lengthy reports of the day's debates. John Wilkes and other heroes of history who fought for the right to report on parliament might wonder what all the fuss was about today.

This unique state of affairs can create the impression of media omnipotence. It reinforces the fashion for blaming the press and the media for the problems that we see played out across it. This in turn leads to the erroneous conclusion that many social problems could be eased or even solved if only something could be done about the press. Some seriously seem to believe that, if only Rupert Murdoch could be driven out of the media business, or preferably out of the country if not off a cliff, then all would surely be well.

Yet the fact that the media has become the dominant arena in public affairs by default does not mean that it runs the world. It is a side effect of the reality created by the broader crisis of public life. If elected politicians appear beholden to the media, does that speak to the power of the press — or the impotence of leaders who lack any public authority of their own? And can the solution really lie in a technical measure to regulate the media, or telling a media mogul he has to quit the market? Or might it have to involve a slightly more profound attempt to revitalise political life with some new visions and inspiring leadership?

The I-blame-the-media reaction is knee-jerk and narrow-minded, too often identifying the wrong problems and solutions. That should not imply that the press is innocent. It has often more than played its part in creating and exacerbating problems. The way that the media has acted in its newly empowered role has had serious internal consequences for standards of journalism, and external ones with regard to, for example, politicians or the police.

In short, the press has not been simply a passive recipient of the crap generated by society. There has also been plenty of effluent pouring back out of the press into the world. The next chapter will sift through some of it.

[1]   The *Guardian*, 29 June 2010.
[2]   *Morning Star*, 15 July 2011.
[3]   *Rolling Stone*, 19 January 2011.
[4]   *Private Eye*, No 1314, 18–31 May 2012.
[5]   Karl Marx, 'On freedom of the press', *Rheinische Zeitung*, No 139, Supplement, 19 May 1842.

6   *City AM*, 25 April 2012.

7   Hugh Grant at the Leveson Inquiry, 21 November 2011 (http://www.levesoninquiry.org.uk/wp-content/uploads/2011/11/Transcript-of-Afternoon-Hearing-21-November-2011.txt).

8   Steve Coogan at the Leveson Inquiry, 22 November 2011 (http://www.levesoninquiry.org.uk/wp-content/uploads/2011/11/Transcript-of-Afternoon-Hearing-22-November-2011.txt).

9   Max Mosley at the Leveson Inquiry, 24 November 2011 (http://www.levesoninquiry.org.uk/wp-content/uploads/2011/11/Transcript-of-Morning-Hearing-24-November-2011.txt).

10 See Daniel J. Boorstin, *The Image: a guide to pseudo-events in America*, Harper and Row 1962.

11 Paul McMullan at the Leveson Inquiry, 29 November 2011 (http://www.levesoninquiry.org.uk/wp-content/uploads/2011/11/Transcript-of-Afternoon-Hearing-29-November-2011.txt).

12 Privacy section, *Stanford Encyclopedia of Philosophy*, http://plato.stanford.edu/entries/privacy; Catharine MacKinnon, *Towards a Feminist Theory of the State*, Harvard University Press 1989.

13 Cited in Mick Hume, *The Times*, 7 October 2005.

14 The *Independent*, 29 April 2012; the *Guardian*, 22 March 2012, 10 July 2012.

15 Quoted in the *Guardian*, 16 March 2012.

16 *The Times*, 20 April 2012.

17 Quoted in the *Daily Mail*, 29 April 2009.

Chapter Five

Here is the News: Journalism as Narcissism

Hard as it may seem to believe, listening to some private phone messages is not the most self-destructive thing that the British press has done in recent years. There has been an extraordinary amount of attention focused on the past crimes of hacking voicemails and of allegedly making illegal payments to policemen and public officials, focused on a couple of tabloid newspapers. Meanwhile other broader and ongoing offences against good journalism across the media have attracted far less attention.

There have been moving and eye-opening stories from the victims of phone-hacking and press intrusion, and some outbreaks of instant amnesia at the Leveson Inquiry that might defy medical opinion. However, probably the most breathtaking revelation I saw reported around the phone-hacking scandal was that the investigation into the hacking of voicemail messages and the related inquiries had become "the biggest police operation in British criminal history". Yes, the biggest police operation in British criminal history. And no, it seems the tabloids were not making it up.

In February 2012 the *Sun*'s outraged associate editor, Trevor Kavanagh, observed that "30 journalists have been needlessly dragged from their beds in dawn raids, arrested and held in police cells while their homes are ransacked" as part of three police investigations into the press that, in terms of numbers of officers involved, he described as Britain's biggest-ever operation, "bigger even than the Pan Am Lockerbie murder probe" into the killing of 270 people in the 1988 terrorist bombing. (We are of course talking here about criminal investigations, not the public order mobilisations involving thousands of officers or the army of police deployed in the 1984–85 miners' strike.)[1]

The following month the Leveson Inquiry heard from deputy mayor of London Kit Malthouse that "27 police were tracking down paedophiles in London, while 150 were working on inquiries into the press". Malthouse, who was Mayor Boris Johnson's man with responsibility for policing and crime in the capital, suggested that by 2013 the number of police staff and officers working on inquiries into the press was forecast to rise to 200 — "the equivalent of eight murder squads".[2]

Which is to say: there were probably rather more detectives probing the fall-out from the hacking of Milly Dowler's voice-mail messages than might have been involved in the search for a missing teenager.

There could hardly be a clearer mark of how central the media has become to Britain's public life. If the press is involved in something, that becomes the story — and the story becomes the biggest news in town. Because of the media's disproportionate influence on our politics and society, whatever it does has an unusual significance. Hence the surreal situation whereby the illicit obtaining of some personal data and official information by a tabloid newspaper can apparently be treated by police as if it were a bigger case than the worst mass murder in British criminal history.

This is symptomatic of how the media has become the story. Once the media reported the news. Now it makes it. From the phone-hacking scandal to rows about press regulation, super-injunctions, leaks, libel and privacy laws, the power of the Murdoch empire and the future of the BBC, the media often seems to be the biggest news around. It is under scrutiny and on trial as never before.

By early 2012 the Leveson Inquiry had become an inquisition into the press and everything it does, alongside a police
operation so intense that a senior journalist could reasonably
call it a witch-hunt. Two of the journalists caught up in the
police investigation had attempted suicide. Yet in an age when
victims are generally treated with compassion and even reverence, there has been little apparent sympathy for those on the
receiving end this time. The tabloid press and journalists are few
people's idea of innocent victims. Some clearly consider that
they have been asking for it.

Those of us determined to defend a free press do not have to
endorse whatever some tabloids have done. But we should
seriously question the legal onslaught. For one thing, because it
is a crime against liberty and history to see the judiciary and the
police closely involved once again in the affairs of a free press.
Nothing good can come of it. Yes, journalists can be held to the
same standards of criminal law as everybody else—but no more
than that, and sometimes less. There should be no selective legal
measures or special police operations against the press, any
more than journalists should automatically be granted immun-
ity. The recent operations appear to have gone some way
beyond investigating specific crimes, to fishing for media offences and meddling in the entire "culture and ethics" of the
press. That sounds like the business of the Thought Police rather
than the Metropolitan branch.

And for another thing, we should question the crackdown
because the narrow legalistic focus on phone-hacking and illicit
payments is confusing the bigger picture about what's wrong
with the UK press. In particular the obsession with phone-
hacking over recent years, an obsession encouraged by the
quality end of the media, has failed to address other more
important problems.

Here is the thing. The apparent belief among some that they
had the right to hack phones as they saw fit was only a symptom of a far bigger affliction, one which has struck not only at
the tabloid press but right across the media. That affliction is
narcissism.

In Greek mythology, Narcissus fell fatally in love with his own reflection, seeing perfection in his image, and perished as a result. When different branches of the media have looked at themselves in recent years they have apparently seen reflected whatever they most cherish. In their own eyes they have sometimes become, not mere reporters and pundits, but the conscience of society, the real opposition to government, the saviours of our children, the liberators of entire nations, the guardians of the planet and all the biodiversity that crawls upon the Earth.

Too often the press believes its own publicity — not surprisingly perhaps, since it also writes the stuff. As a result journalists have sometimes become caught up in a sense of their own power and self-importance. They have turned into crusaders. And editors and reporters on a crusade have sometimes convinced themselves that they can do anything they want in the name of righteousness — including hacking the phone messages of the innocent. As with Narcissus, the media obsession with itself is a dangerous and self-destructive one.

The curse of narcissism stems from the way in which the media has become so central to public life. As discussed in the previous section, the press has acquired this increased influence largely by default, through the withering of other political and public institutions. Nevertheless, its new status has fed some delusions of grandeur at the court of king media. The press and other news media have assumed a role in politics and society that is not part of their proper function. The way this has evolved has had serious adverse consequences not only for those dealing with the media but for journalism too.

Not everything that is wrong with the UK press and wider media is down to outside influences, whether that be devious PR agents or the internet. Not every restriction on the freedom and openness of the press is a product of legal injustice or state persecution. There have been important internal developments in the conduct of the media and journalism in recent times that have helped to create the current crisis. These trends have been amplified by the inflated status which the media now occupies in public life.

The press is a reflection of what is going on in wider society. But it is not a passive recipient of cultural trends and practices. There might be plenty of ordure flowing into the media from society, notably from the political elites. But there is also some important and malodorous stuff flowing in the other direction, out of the media into society—and we are not only talking here about the obvious targets among the popular press. Defending the freedom of the press as an absolute principle need not mean ignoring the abuses of that freedom. It should, however, mean not simply focusing on the usual suspects.

Some of the new ways in which the press and the wider media have operated of late have been bad for our culture and our politics. They have also been bad for journalism and for those who wish to see it flourish in the future. The media is in danger of discarding some important traditions and values and replacing them with nothing much.

Look at some of what the narcissistic press is guilty of today—but which it is too rarely criticised for, or only in superficial fashion. The key to all of this lies in the new default position of power the media enjoys amid the ruins of our political system and public life.

The New Crusaders

It sometimes seems that the media has become so much the centre of everything in public life that nothing—not even an election or war—can really be said to have happened if it does not command constant media coverage.

As a result of its newly elevated status, some among the media appear to have acquired a sense of self-importance. Any story that involves the media itself will quickly become big news—which is why phone-hacking and the Leveson Inquiry became the biggest story around, despite considerable public indifference. Moreover, even where the news has nothing ostensibly to do with the media, there is a tendency for some reporters to act as if it had and put themselves at the centre of the story.

This narcissism can take over entire newspapers, at either end of the "quality" spectrum. The tabloid *News of the World* became famously obsessive about posing as the saviour of children everywhere in its crusade for "Sarah's Law", which would allow people to find out about convicted sex offenders in their area. The paper elected itself as representative of the public and people's avenger, plastering sex offenders' photos on its front page and demanding that the government did as it was told.

But other media outlets have suffered just as inflated delusions of grandeur. Around the turn of the millennium, with New Labour in its pomp and the Tory Party in complete disarray, some broadsheet and BBC editors decided that the media must step in and become the "real opposition" to Tony Blair. In September 2000 the UK's leading liberal paper published and distributed thousands of copies of its very own *Guardian Manifesto*. An editorial boasted that this was "unprecedented in United Kingdom journalism" and that its "bold, new ideas" should "stimulate a vigorous, enjoined discussion about not only the future of the government—but the future of the country".[3] Sadly the public failed to be invigorated by or join the "vigorous, enjoined discussion" and the notion of a newspaper handing down a manifesto to shape "the future of the country" sank without trace. More sadly still, the press's inflated ego did not go with it.

Today there is a self-righteous school of reporting whose adherents act not as simple journalists, and not even as crusading journalists, but as if they were genuine Crusaders on a moral mission to save the world from evil. This is often clearest in foreign and war reporting. Reporters feel freer to indulge their crusader fantasies in the middle of somebody else's war. From the 1990s, while the tabloids launched a crusade against the inflated threat posed by "paedos" to our children, other media crusaders embarked on a global campaign to save the children of the world from various incarnations of the "new Nazis".

It's as if somebody has hacked into their brains and set their worldview to "Manichean", where every conflict can be reduced to a fairy tale-type struggle between the forces of Good and Evil. So the crusaders scour the globe searching for something evil, against which they can pose on the moral high ground. The more each new evil can be depicted as Hitlerian or genocidal, the better the light in which they can cast themselves.

The turning point in opening the age of the crusaders was the civil wars in the former Yugoslavia during the 1990s. Many British and Western reporters turned the conflict in Bosnia into a simple morality play, reducing the political complexities of a civil war to a black-and-white battle against Evil. They often compared the "evil" Serbs to the Nazis, with journalists themselves cast in the role of leading the resistance to genocide—rhetorically at least. Many served as "laptop bombardiers" who fired off articles demanding that NATO bomb the Serbs on their instructions.

These crusaders disguised as reporters, as I wrote in a pamphlet back then, were conducting "a moral mission on behalf of a demoralised society":

> "At a time when many in the West are unsure about the meaning of right and wrong, war reporters are trying to re-establish some moral certainties in relation to faraway places. In launching their mission to vanquish 'evil' in Bosnia or Rwanda, they are using other people's life and death conflicts to work out their own existential angst, turning the world's war zones into private battlegrounds where troubled journalists can fight for their own souls by playing the role of crusader."[4]

After NATO followed the crusaders' orders and bombed the Bosnian Serbs, BBC correspondent Martin Bell called for a new school of war reporting—"the journalism of attachment... a journalism that cares as well as knows". War reporters, said Bell, are "no longer spectators, but participants", with a responsibility and the power to take sides with good against evil and demand of the international community that "something-must-

be-done".[5] Around the same time as Bell was extolling the virtues of war journalism as a fighter for good, one American
correspondent hailed the idea of a global "Government of the
International Media" as a force for world peace, concluding that
it "does have a great ring to it".[6] Not only were reporters now to
be "participants" in other people's wars, naturally on the side of
Good, but some apparently considered them capable of teach-
ing the world to sing in perfect harmony.

Fifteen years later I doubt if any serious foreign correspondent would endorse Bell's explicit call for a journalism of attachment. Yet it sometimes seems that many of them now practise it
anyway. From Kosovo in 1999 through Iraq in 2003 to Libya in
2011, Western journalists have often banged the drum for war
louder than anybody else.

No international crisis appears complete these days without
some journalists pursuing what Americans sometimes call the I-
was-there school of personalised reporting, putting themselves
and their feelings at the centre of the story in order to make an
emotive case for international intervention. In February 2012,
when the courageous veteran war reporter Marie Colvin of the
Sunday Times was killed along with a French photo-journalist by
a government shell in a rebel area of Syria, one of the other
foreign journalists injured at the time announced to the international press that "I need a ceasefire". Sometimes I-was-there
can sound more like look-at-me.[7]

Since Crusaders are dealing with a black-and-white world,
there is inevitably a tendency to take sides in the conflicts. During 2011, *Sky News* ran a series of short promo films celebrating
the role of their reporters in the Libyan civil war where rebels
backed by NATO bombing overthrew the regime of Colonel
Gadaffi. In one film the reporter says that, after the leader of the
rebel group they were with was killed, the emotional Sky crew
felt they wanted to leave them to grieve in private, but decided,
no: "they had a story to tell and we were there to tell it." The
idea of top TV news reporters revealing their emotional attach-
ments, and declaring that their job is to tell the story of one side
in a civil war, seems a departure from the treasured traditions of

(attempted) journalistic objectivity in mainstream war reporting. Award-winning war reporters Ed Vulliamy of the *Observer* and Lindsey Hilsum of *Channel 4 News* have abandoned notions of neutrality and given evidence for the prosecution at international war crimes trials, effectively crossing the line that traditionally separates reporters from police informants.

Once you start acting as a crusader rather than simply a journalist, there is a danger that you see what you want to see and stop asking the sort of critical questions that ought to be your stock in trade. Thus it was that so many journalists and editors on both sides of the Atlantic too readily swallowed the line about Saddam Hussein's supposed Weapons of Mass Destruction that was put forward by President George W. Bush and Prime Minister Tony Blair in support of the 2003 invasion of Iraq. Despite the absence of any credible or substantive evidence of the non-existent WMDs in Blair's "dodgy dossier", many in the media were predisposed to join in another crusade against an evil Iraqi regime which the Bush administration declared to be worse that Hitler or Stalin. When the absence of WMDs became clear after the US-UK invasion, reporters and politicians complained that they had been "duped" into supporting the disastrous war. It would be truer to say that many had deluded themselves in pursuit of another self-righteous crusade.

The big question remains, why have so many serious journalists apparently decided that it is their job not just to report on conflicts, but to take sides and demand more forceful outside intervention? Not only to analyse and explain the world, but to try to save it?

It is of course natural to be moved by the sight of human suffering in wars around the world. It is also entirely legitimate to discuss how the UK and the West should respond to crises, and to debate the pros and cons of intervention. Some of us remain ardent anti-interventionists. First on the ground of principle—that it is not the business of Britain or any Western power to determine the future for other peoples. And also on the ground of practicality—because experience from A for Afghanistan to Y for Yugoslavia suggests that attempts to "liberate" others on their behalf or import democracy by force tend to end in debacle or disaster. Other observers are perfectly entitled to take a different view of the merits of intervention.

The trouble is that the new class of media crusaders are not really engaged in a debate about what intervention might mean for those who are meant to be delivered from evil. Instead the media crusaders have developed a habit of making other people's wars seem to be all about "us". The laptop bombardiers writing from home are the worst. Every international crisis since Bosnia has to be described as "the test of our generation", and we are warned it will be a "national shame" if we fail to intervene against the new Nazis.

One newspaper pundit demanding intervention in Syria in 2012 confirmed that, in spite of what one might assume, the issue was less about Them, the actual Syrian people, than it was actually about Us. He declared that we must show our moral superiority to "fascism" (that is, the repressive Assad regime): "We're better than that and in our actions we will show it." And even if Western intervention resulted in greater "chaos" in Syria, he assured us, "It is important to add weight to our moral impulse". No matter what the consequences for the Syrians might be in terms of adding to the chaos, the important thing was to show the world Britain's "moral impulse" with some "weight" — bombs? — behind it. Military intervention — war — is here apparently recast as a token of our strong feelings, as expressed by journalists acting as society's self-appointed conscience.[8]

The BBC reporter Fergal Keane became famous for his emotional reports from Rwanda, published under the revealing title *Letter to Daniel: Despatches From the Heart*, in which he combined a highly personal account of the 1994 massacres with his hopes as a father that his young son might grow up in a better world. Mixing the roles of parent and reporter in this way, Keane managed effectively to make his feelings the focus in the midst of a terrible civil conflict. As one sympathetic account explains, "According to Keane such personalisation of the genocide was necessary because it is impossible to explain brutalities in numbers or artificial terms like 'massacre' or 'genocide'. 'They [the audience] just don't get it. It is too big.'"[9] It seems that journalist crusaders feel they have to display their tears and terrors because the rest of us "just don't get" the "artificial" things such as facts and words of three syllables. After *Letter to Daniel* made him a media celebrity, Keane wrote about feeling "exhilarated, flattered, amused and frightened" suddenly to find himself the centre of attention—but also noted the danger of foreign reporters getting a taste for the spotlight, to the point where "journalism becomes secondary or a mere tool in the business of sustaining one's celebrity".[10]

My 1997 pamphlet about the dangers of the journalism of attachment was called *Whose War is it Anyway?* That would seem a question still worth asking of those Western journalists who appear so vain they sometimes imagine that somebody else's life and death conflict is about them. Because their crusades tend to be focused on what intervention will mean for Us in the West, it does not seem to matter so much that international interventions from Kosovo to Iraq have generally ended in something less than triumph for the peoples on the receiving end. Crusaders can pack up their laptops and satellite phones and helicopter on to the next crisis in some faraway place of which we know little, carrying the White Journalist's Burden in their backpack.

The narcissism and emotionalism of the overseas crusaders reporting on foreign wars or the war against global warming has long since been re-imported to domestic news coverage. Whether it is reporters telling us how they feel about big stories they are covering, or the sort of self-privacy-invading "personal" columns that seem to fill newspaper supplements, journalists are often at the centre of things. Some might think this can be a good thing, breaking down the old barriers of the press-public divide and trying to make an emotional connection with an audience in a new way. But the fashion for putting feelings ahead of hard facts and swapping sentimentality for seriousness can also have a less "soft" side.

There is often a current of Emotional Correctness in the new emotionalism of the media, telling us how we ought to feel about events in no uncertain terms. A turning point came with the massacre of 16 Scottish schoolchildren and their teacher at a school in Dunblane, Scotland, in 1996, when respected BBC correspondent Kate Adie was told off by her bosses for being too "forensic" in her reports of the killings — that is, focusing too much on the evidence and providing an insufficient effusion of emotion to guide her audience's response.

Things reached a new peak (or low) the following year around the death of Diana, Princess of Wales, when the media helped to orchestrate a national grief fest and broadcast nothing but expressions of ersatz emotion for a week, culminating in the day of her funeral. The *Daily Mirror* instructed its readers to ensure that, when thinking of the funeral, they would remember "how you felt and what Diana meant to you and the world". In case you were in any doubt as to how you should feel and what Diana ought to mean to you, the *Mirror* printed a subtle reminder in the shape of a two-page feature on the coming funeral, headlined "BE SILENT ALL BRITAIN".[11] Journalists from every department seemed to fill every newspaper with morally instructive tales of how they felt they "knew" the princess and what her death meant to them. Diana was "a woman who meant so much to the world. Especially me" announced the *Sun*'s sensitive motoring correspondent, Jeremy Clarkson.[12] Meanwhile the BBC brought its famous confessional reporter Fergal Keane back from overseas to give a broken-voiced commentary on the funeral. In a biting critique of Keane's modus operandi, one commentator pointed out that "The danger of this type of journalism is that the reporter becomes more important than the event he or she is covering, and what matters is not what happened but how it affected the observer. Not only that, the response is prescribed for the reader: we are told how we ought to feel".[13] The reporter, in other words, risks becoming a cross between a psychoanalyst and a preacher.

The coverage of Diana's death and funeral has provided the template for a series of "Princess Diana moments" over the subsequent 15 years. The pattern is for the media to repeat the same thing over and again in an emotionally shaky voice — these days backed up by a chorus on Twitter. Anybody who appears to dissent from the code of Emotional Correctness risks being effectively outlawed. Examples range from the 2007 disappearance of, and subsequent hunt for, young Madeleine McCann; in May 2012, five years after she disappeared from her family's holiday apartment, the *Sun* could still make an "OUT-RAGE" front page story out of a charlatan psychic claiming the spirits had told him she was dead:[14] to the 2012 collapse of Bolton footballer Fabrice Muamba on the pitch at Tottenham; a drunken Swansea student who pilloried Muamba on Twitter was not only hounded by tweeters but reported to police, prosecuted, jailed for 56 days and kicked off his university course.

In these and many other instances, the media is feeding us emotional pills to dictate how we should feel. The assumption often appears to be that we simple folk could not feel humanity towards a missing child or a young sportsman and father suffering a cardiac arrest unless we are guided by their code of Emotional Correctness.

The self-importance and self-righteousness of the emotion-ally high media sometimes seems to know no bounds. There are moments when they can sacrifice all notions of journalism to become something else, crusaders getting carried away with their self-styled cause. That is surely what happened with phone-hacking at the *News of the World*, a symptom of the prob-lem of narcissism, where a reporter can stand up and say that he thinks he has the right to hack anybody's phone because "priv-acy is for paedos" and he is on a mission to catch "bad people". On the other side, there have been signs of a similar anything-goes-in-a-good-cause attitude in the crusade to punish the tab-loid press over phone-hacking, reporting sensational stories as fact — most notably the revelation that the *News of the World* had deleted key messages from missing Milly Dowler's phone, a revelation which led directly to the closure of the paper and the setting up of the Leveson Inquiry, yet turned out to be unsub-stantiated. Never mind, the crusaders got the grail.

Operating as a crusader more than a journalist there is always a danger of seeing what you want to see rather than all that is there. The question of objectivity in news reporting has long been a thorny one. Nobody would pretend that it is easy to remain objective when reporting on divisive and moving issues. However, objectivity has at least been recognised as a goal to be striven for, if not always attained. Otherwise we might as well call ourselves poets or playwrights rather than reporters. Until now, that is, when one symptom of the creeping narcissism in the media is a growing sense that journalistic objectivity, and the ability to view awkward facts dispassionately, is not only unattainable, but arguably undesirable anyway.

At the extreme this approach can even lead crusaders to invent the truth, all in a good cause. Tabloid newspapers are often accused of operating according to the maxim "why let the facts get in the way of a good story?" If so, they are not alone. The plagiarism and fabrication scandals that have rocked quality newspapers on both sides of the Atlantic in recent years, from the *New York Times* to the *Independent* in London, are in part symptoms of the same scourge of narcissism among crusaders. After all, if you know beyond doubt that you are Right and on the side of Good, does it really matter if you get the facts badly wrong? A few years back a top journalist even felt able to write an article in praise of "the good lie", saying of the British government's wild scaremongering over the threat of a heterosexual Aids epidemic that "The government has lied — and I am glad".[15]

Outright cases of plagiarism or fabrication remain thankfully rare in our generally honest media. Perhaps a more general symptom of the changes in journalism is the way that comment and opinion have not only expanded in the press, but increasingly become mixed up with news coverage. There is nothing wrong with comment and opinion writing; it is a vital part of the "national conversation", and what some of us mostly do. It has always been recognised, however, that the free-for-all of opinions should be kept as separate as possible from the objective search for facts in reporting. In the classic formulation put forward by the most famous editor of the *Guardian*, C.P. Scott, "Comment is free, but facts are sacred". In the age of media narcissism and the journalist-as-crusader, both sides of that principle seem to be at some risk. There is a danger that comment, whilst proliferating, can become more conformist and less free under the codes of Emotional Correctness. And at the same time that the sacredness of facts can be at risk of sacrifice on the altar of the latest crusade, whether that be against "paedos", Nazis or phone-hacking hacks.

It remains the case that the media reflects the real world rather than ruling it. But it is also assuming a role that has nothing to do with its proper function, dominating public discussion and acting as a crusader. That can explain both why the outbreak of phone-hacking happened in the first place—and why such a media-centric affair somehow became the biggest news story going.

The consequences of this for a free and open press, serious journalism and objective reporting have been far-reaching. There is an old rhyme, written by Humbert Wolfe, that has been used a lot in coverage of the phone-hacking scandal and the Leveson Inquiry:

> "You cannot hope to bribe or twist,
> thank God! the British journalist.
> But, seeing what the man will do
> unbribed, there's no occasion to"

It is normally quoted today to illustrate how lowlife tabloid journalism has supposedly become. It could, however, readily be applied to the apparently unimpeachable high-minded journalism of the quality media, when you see what some crusaders have proved willing to do in pursuit of a pet cause at home or abroad.

There is a tendency today to blame the difficulties in journalism on market pressures and the cuts brought on by the decline of newspapers and the economic recession. Those are all big problems. But the problematic tendencies referred to here predated the recession, and have more to do with the culture than the economics of reporting the news.

The Fatal Embrace with the Political Elite

How are we to make sense of these unhealthy developments in journalism? The new narcissism of the press is directly conn- ected to the position of unprecedented influence that the media enjoys in public life today. One aspect that has come in for a lot of criticism of late has been the close relationship between leading politicians and media executives. Even here, however, much of the criticism is missing the bigger target.

The Leveson Inquiry turned an embarrassingly bright light on the political elite's links with the Rupert Murdoch media empire, under both the New Labour governments of Tony Blair and Gordon Brown and then the Conservative-Lib Dem coal- ition government led by David Cameron. Yet like much else in politics today, the focus has been too narrowly on the personal. We heard mind-numbing details about precisely how many times prime ministers and politicians met or had dinner with the media moguls and press men. There have been demands for forensic dissection of the emails and text messages between ministers and their special advisors and Murdoch executives and their minions.

These gossipy obsessions reached their nadir in "Horse- gate", the manure-fuelled scandal over whether or not there had been something corrupt about former *Sun* and *News of the World* editor and News International chief executive Rebekah Brooks being allowed to look after a retired police horse, and worse, whether or not David Cameron had actually sat on said nag during a visit to the Brooks' home. A nod, as the old saying goes, being as good as a wink to a blind horse, or indeed a one- eyed tabloid-basher. Things got even more serious when it was sensationally revealed not only that the prime minister sent Ms Brooks text messages ending LOL, but that he thought this stood for Lots Of Love rather than Laughing Out Loud.

If this is what passes for serious political criticism we should not be surprised to find the whole world LOL at us. Hard as it may seem to accept, there are even bigger questions that should be posed here than counting dinners and emails or tracking horse rides, swims, text messages and who had a drink with

whom. Questions such as, for example: why have British politicians become so dependent upon their relationship with the
media? And how did "spin" replace argument as the currency
of our political life?

It is the crisis of authority suffered by the other institutions,
notably parliament and the political parties, that has put the
media at the centre of public affairs. This has had some far-
reaching consequences. Political leaders without the reliable
party machines and solid constituencies of the past have had to
look to the media to get their message across. They have
nowhere else to go. Hence the media event has replaced the
public meeting or political rally as a way of addressing the electorate. At the same time, parties that have lost touch with the
electorate and seen their roots in society shrivel fear that the
media can exercise an influence over voters that is beyond them
as politicians. Hence winning friends in high places within the
media has become seen as even more important by political
leaders. With the withering of the political sphere, the media
has loomed larger and larger over it.

But what is new about all this? Everybody knows that links
between top politicians and press barons have long been close.
Of late, however, we have been looking at a different sort of
relationship, reflecting changes in the status of both the media
and political elites.

Since the birth of mass democracy in the nineteenth century,
British political parties have always sought to win a favourable
hearing in the press. During much of the Victorian era it was
common enough for parties to back their own newspapers, or
perhaps to patronise journalists to put their line across. With the
explosion of mass newspapers at the end of the nineteenth
century, politicians became keen to establish relations with the
press barons who owned them as a conduit for reaching the
newly enfranchised class of voters.

Men such as Lord Rothermere, Lord Beaverbrook and Lord
Northcliffe became powerful figures as publishers of the *Daily
Mirror*, *Daily Express* and *Daily Mail*. The megalomaniac Lord
Copper, Evelyn Waugh's fictional newspaper baron in *Scoop*

(1938) was said to be an amalgam of Lords Northcliffe and Beaverbrook. The battle for sales and influence between Lord Copper's *Daily Beast* and Lord Zinc's *Daily Brute* mirrored the real one between the *Mail* and the *Express*.

The search for political influence was not restricted to the "popular" press. The current editor of the *Guardian* advised Lord Justice Leveson that previous editors of his paper had also enjoyed cosy relations with prime ministers. "Alastair Hetherington, my predecessor, used to have almost weekly meetings with [Labour prime minister] Harold Wilson. [First World War Liberal PM David] Lloyd George used to run his Cabinet changes past [*Guardian* editor] C.P. Scott before he did them, so I don't think this is a new problem."[16]

The old press barons exercised direct political power in a way denied to their successors. Lord Beaverbrook of the *Express* served as a British government minister of information during the First World War, and as Winston Churchill's minister of war production during the Second World War, accompanying Churchill to summit meetings with US President Franklin D. Roosevelt. So far as we know, nobody has yet suggested inviting current *Express* owner Richard Desmond to run the Ministry of Defence or go schmoozing with Cameron and President Barack Obama.

In the past, however, these close relations were on a different footing. Both the politicians and the press barons had their own independent views of the world and sources of authority. Politicians represented parties and clear constituencies with distinctive political outlooks and interests. The newspaper owners too had their own firm political agendas, and were not solely chasing sales and advertising money. It would be hard to imagine a newspaper today taking such a controversial stand as the *Daily Mail*'s infamous headline "Hurrah for the Blackshirts", on an article Lord Rothermere himself wrote praising Oswald Mosley's British Union of Fascists in 1934, which described Mosley's outfit as "a well organised party of the right ready to take over responsibility for national affairs with the same direct- ness of purpose and energy of method as Hitler and Mussolini have displayed", and ended with a call for young men to apply to join the Blackshirts at their HQ in King's Road, Chelsea.[17]

These independently authoritative politicians and press barons were also more than capable of falling out. In 1931 Beaverbrook and Rothermere sought to oust Stanley Baldwin as the leader of the Conservative Party. Baldwin turned on his newspaper critics in a speech that has rung down the ages: "What the proprietorship of these papers [the *Mail* and the *Express*] is aiming at is power," he declared, "but power without responsibility, the prerogative of the harlot throughout the ages." Baldwin won that tussle with the harlots of the press and went on to serve as prime minister for a third time between 1935 and 1937.[18]

So why did the always-important though often-troubled relationship between the powers of the press and political worlds turn into something different and apparently closer over the past 15 years or so? It was not because the press somehow grew more powerful. It was more because both sides of that power relationship lost their independent outlook and authority, and were reduced to clinging together more tightly for succour and survival.

The problems are clearest in relation to the political parties. In recent decades we have seen the end of the era of traditional Left vs. Right politics, and an accompanying decline of party memberships, solid constituencies and safe parliamentary seats on all sides. Isolated party leaders have increasingly turned to the media, seeing it as their only way to connect with voters and get their message across in the absence of dynamic party outlets of their own.

By the time Tony Blair became its leader in 1994, the Labour Party was an empty and outdated shell. Blair's team presented him as a presidential-style national figure to compensate, projecting a showbiz personal image to hide the hole where his party was supposed to be. With the party reduced to little more than a leader with a PR campaign, Blair became dependent on the media to publicise his New Labour brand. That was why he made a beeline for the Murdoch media machine from the start, flying around the world to address a top News Corporation conference in 1995. Two years later the *Sun* endorsed Blair in the 1997 general election, where New Labour won a landslide victory.

The withering of traditional political parties and subsequent turn to the media also helps to explain how "spin" became the first language of politics. For politicians concerned with PR rather than principles, what you might stand for becomes less important than how any policy might "play" in the press. Blair's chief spin doctor, Alastair Campbell, became notorious for allegedly manipulating the media. However, these trends raised the question of exactly who was spinning who. When policy is apparently driven by the search for headlines, and governments seem keen to declare new laws and initiatives in response to any passing splash in the press, it can appear that the media is calling the shots and the politicians are more spun than spinning.

The turn to the media did not end with Blair and New Labour. When he became Conservative leader in 2005 David Cameron declared that the age of New Labour spin and headline-chasing politics was over. Yet before long Cameron, a PR man by profession before going into politics, had adopted the same media-centric approach out of necessity. His "modernising" team saw the dwindling Tory Party membership as an anachronistic and dysfunctional embarrassment, much as the New Labour leadership had viewed the rump of old Labour activists. Cameron went to great lengths to get the media onside, flying by private jet for an audience with Murdoch and then hiring Andy Coulson, who had resigned as *News of the World* editor over phone-hacking, as his chief spin doctor. It was widely viewed as significant when the *Sun*, albeit without much enthusiasm, went over to the Tories from Labour before the 2010 election—not least by Labour Prime Minister Gordon Brown, who was reportedly apoplectic at this "betrayal" by his most valued supporters. Nor has the Tories' media-chasing been confined to the Murdoch press. In May 2012 it was revealed that Conservative government ministers had met Google executives 23 times since entering government—an average of one meeting every month. Presumably the ministers were not looking for advice on how to search for cheap insurance online.

(The crisis of political institutions also explains, incidentally, why UK parties seem to be caught up in repeated financial scandals involving rich donors. They lack the active memberships and loyal support to raise a lot of money. Yet for the same reasons, they need more cash than ever to pay for the media campaigns on which they must rely. Thus party leaders chase after big donors to compensate, in the same way that they turn to big media as a substitute for mass memberships.)

The recent embrace between the press and political elites has been a response to a crisis of authority in UK society rather than simply personal predilection or profit-seeking. If you want further proof of that, ask a policeman. It is a sign of the general institutional crisis at work here that the British police too have been playing the same game, cosying up to the media in a bid to win more public approval.

There had been a fairly close relationship between the British police force and the modern newspapers ever since they both emerged during the nineteenth century. The papers always valued splashing the inside details of gory murders and other crimes, while for their part the police would look to the press to convey their public appeals and polish their standing as the "thin blue line" protecting civilisation. In the 1950s and 1960s TV shows such as *Dixon of Dock Green* and *Z-Cars* were great propaganda for the ideal of a public-friendly force "policing by consent". In practical terms the two-way exchange of information between the press and police was always an important part of both operations.

In more recent times this relationship also moved on to a different phase. Police chiefs, like politicians, have become more insecure, fearing a loss of popular consent for their force in the face of riots, scandals and embarrassing revelations about everything from racism to sleaze. They too turned to the media in the hope of projecting a more "user-friendly" image and connecting with the public, employing every media device from *Crime-*

watch-style TV shows to Facebook pages appealing for information during a murder investigation.

We have witnessed the rise of the phenomenon of PR policing, in which trying to capture the correct media image of the police has often seemed at least as important as catching criminals. In fact during major operations, notably emotive cases such as murders or child abductions, it sometimes seems as if there are two parallel policing operations taking place — a secretive pursuit of intelligence and suspects, alongside a high-profile campaign of PR policing involving emotional press conferences and public appeals. Meanwhile no major police raid or operation has seemed complete in recent years without an accompanying camera crew and press team. The unusual thing about the dawn arrests of journalists over phone-hacking and illicit payments, apart from the heavy-handedness involved, was the absence of other journalists accompanying the police to photograph and write up the story in melodramatic style.

A Closed Oligarchy

The incestuous-looking relationship between the media and the political elite in recent years has created the impression of an increasingly powerful press. At the same time, however, the media has paid a heavy price for its elevation. There were negative consequences for journalism even before the phone-hacking scandal brought matters to a head. The creeping affliction of narcissism across the media was one. Another has been the closing of the media mind, as it becomes part of a new cut-off oligarchy at the top of society.

From politicians to police chiefs, the isolated pillars of what would once have been called the British establishment have turned to the media that they see as their only way to make a connection and get a message across. This has led to all of the scandalised discussion of late about how the powerful press has been corrupting politics and the police.

There is a danger, however, of missing the other side of the story. The "powerful" press has not been immune to the crisis of authority in UK institutions. The media is just as anchorless and disoriented as the other great institutions today, adrift in a changing society and fearful of losing its audience and its roots in the marketplace. Many at the top of the media have become as keen as defensive politicians or police chiefs to make friends in high places. They have ended up clinging together for succour as part of a new isolated and insulated political-media class.

The press certainly seems to have more clout than ever before amid the withering of the British establishment, the media emerging as the last pillar standing in public life. But they have acquired that influence more by accident than intentionality. The pervasiveness of the media in public and political affairs should not be mixed up with any "Murdoch and media moguls run the country" fantasies.

It is arguable that the press barons of the past actually came closer to the image of powerful and manipulative political players than the media chiefs of today. In the 1920s and 1930s the likes of Rothermere, Beaverbrook and North tended to pursue clear political agendas and had close relations with the party leaders, particularly the Tory Party. They supported and promoted definite programmes and politicians that shared their strident views of the world.

By contrast much of the media today stands for little if anything at all. It more often seems that the press and other media are trying to say whatever they think people want to hear— rather like contemporary politicians. The media elite no longer sees its role as cultivating public opinion or pushing people in a particular direction. They are much more concerned about advertising, finding niche markets, getting an audience to identify with them and not putting off too many people. In this sense the role model for the modern media executive is less Lord Copper, more Simon Cowell. There is also a distinct absence of clear old-fashioned political values being pushed in the media today. Instead somebody like Rupert Murdoch has gained a reputation for backing winners by spotting which way the current of public opinion is already flowing, and nimbly changing horses midstream where necessary. Such astute opportunism seems some way from being a "puppet master" controlling political events to suit a particular end or agenda.

The political, media and state elites were drawn closer together over recent decades in response to their common loss of public authority and roots. As a result they have formed a new entity in UK public life: a closed oligarchy, cut off from society as never before. There has been a lot of focus of late on the damage this drawing together of the elites has done to politics—although the complaints are often trivial and too personalised, and mistake the symptoms of the unpopularity of politics for its cause. But if anything the damage done to the press and the media has been rather worse.

The press has lost too much of the independence it once enjoyed from the political class and instead become an integral part of the corporate elite. The media might appear more powerful compared to the past, albeit by default. But it is also less free, especially in the sense of being open. Oligarchy is anathema to the ideals of a free press and freedom of expression. As media organisations have become fused into the new elite, we have witnessed a closing of the media mind. Just as the terrain of political debate has narrowed with the end of Left vs. Right, so has the media agenda become more limited and conformist. There are, for example, more newspaper columnists and bloggers than ever before—arguably often expressing fewer distinctive opinions and political outlooks on anything more important than their personal lives.

Falling Out

All in all then, the media's newly elevated position in public life has not done the press any favours. Its integration into a closed oligarchy has made it less free in terms of openness. And its appearance of power has encouraged delusions of grandeur and narcissism, sending the press off in directions that have little to do with the job of unearthing and reporting the news. There has often seemed to be a heavy price to pay in terms of journalism for the privilege of being a power in the land.

Now matters have got worse. As the political and media elites have fallen out around the Leveson Inquiry, politicians and the police have been trying to reassert their authority by turning on their erstwhile allies in the press. Those who were accused of being "too cosy" with the Murdoch media empire have sought to distance themselves and display their independence by giving News Corp a good kicking. The result has been the Leveson Inquiry into the press, set up by Tory prime minister and former Murdoch ally David Cameron with the support of former Murdoch sleepover pals in the Labour Party, and the massive police operation to investigate phone-hacking and illicit payments by the press, launched by the same Met force that until recently enjoyed convivial relations with the Murdoch press.

Liberal Democrat business secretary Vince Cable might have got into trouble after he was secretly recorded boasting that he had "declared war on Mr Murdoch". But the loose-lipped Cable was only letting slip what had become the unofficial war policy of many in the political class.[19]

The irony is that these attempts to take the press down a peg or two hundred have confirmed the media's central role in public life. Thus phone-hacking and the rest has become the biggest news around, repeatedly shoving financial crises, wars and even footballers and reality shows set in Essex out of the headlines. There has even been mad talk of how the Leveson Inquiry could save British democracy—by taming the tabloid press and banishing the Murdochs. To have any effect on public perceptions today, the authorities' revenge against the press has to be carried out in the full glare of media coverage, otherwise it wouldn't have happened. The largely supine media has gone along with this and made the humiliation of the popular press top news.

There is little sign of public sympathy for the journalists and executives caught up in this official backlash. But we should be worried about the effect it might have on the future struggle for a free press.

Many concerns have been expressed about 'unhealthy' and 'too close' relations between senior police officers and the Murdoch press. Yet those concerns are being exploited to justify a more dangerous relationship, one where rather than the media poking around in police business, the Met take a close interest in the affairs of the press—with the collaboration of newspaper management and the support of crusading journalists.

Scotland Yard was badly embarrassed by criticism of the Met's early conduct of the phone-hacking investigation, and revelations about links to the press which led to the resignation of its commissioner. Since then the Met's new leadership has been trying to reassert the Force's moral authority by pursuing a zealous campaign against the wicked tabloids that allegedly besmirched the honour of naïve and innocent police chiefs.

It was in this surreal atmosphere that the police war on hacking phone messages and buying information from public officials became the largest-scale investigation in British criminal history, with leading *Sun* journalists arrested in dawn raids while police squads tore up their floorboards. Meanwhile News Corp's own Management and Standards Committee was busy tearing up the book on protecting journalists and their sources, by handing over millions of emails and internal documents to the Met and setting up the *Sun's* own people for arrest. So much for the "ethical" backlash against bad practice in the press.

Whatever problems there are in the media today will not be solved by the police taking a closer interest in the affairs of a free press. Nor by a judge ruling on what is and is not the "ethical" way to exercise freedom of expression. Or by government ministers devising new rules to regulate the limits of what we should be allowed to write, publish and read.

The media itself needs to reassess its role. One idea that might help would be if journalists adopted an approach that was a little more humble—and at the same time one that took journalism more seriously. Humble in the sense of accepting that reporters are not crusaders on a mission to save the world and its children. Yet more serious in the sense of recognising that journalism is far too important to be reduced to an outpouring of personal emotions or private confessionals or regurgitated PR puff and starry tweets or wiki-leaked gossip. Journalism has an important job to do in informing public debate, arming people with both the evidence and the arguments to conduct an honest discussion and make decisions about where our society is heading. That has never seemed a more urgent task than today, when the economic crisis is being exacerbated by the crisis of political thinking and fresh ideas.

The time is right for a more free, open and independent media that can break away from the problems of the recent past. Such a break was never going to be easy to make. But it will be harder still if we allow the response to the problems of the press to be dictated by the elites hiding behind Lord Justice Leveson, who want to purge the press of whatever they disapprove of and close things down even more. The new danger journalism faces in all this is not censorship by a police state. It is an ever-more closed atmosphere of conformism. Who needs the police to control the press when so many now seem prepared to toe the Leveson line?

1   The *Sun*, 13 February 2012.
2   Quoted in *The Times*, 30 March 2012.
3   The *Guardian*, 25 September 2000.
4   Mick Hume, 'Whose war is it anyway?: The dangers of the journalism of attachment', *Junius*, 2007.
5   Martin Bell, 'TV news: How far should we go?', *British Journalism Review*, Vol 8 No 1, 1997.
6   Peter Arnett, 'The clash of arms in exotic locales', *Media Studies Journal*, Autumn 1996.
7   Quoted in *The Times*, 24 February 2012.
8   *The Times*, 24 February 2012.
9   Cited in 'Screaming in silence', *Whyze*, April 2005 (www.whyze.eu).
10 The *Guardian*, 23 June 2012.
11 The *Daily Mirror*, 2 September 1997.
12 The *Sun*, 2 September 1997.
13 The *Independent on Sunday*, 19 October 1997.
14 The *Sun*, 15 May 2012.
15 Mark Lawson, the *Guardian*, 24 June 1996.
16 Quoted in *The Times*, 18 January 2012.
17 The *Daily Mail*, 15 January 1934.

18   Philip Williamson and Edward Baldwin (eds.), *Baldwin Papers: A Conservative Statesman, 1908–1947*, Cambridge University Press 2004, p. 258.
19   *Daily Telegraph*, 21 December 2010.

Chapter Six

Leveson's Mission –
Purging the Press

"You must understand, sir, that a person is either with this court or he must be counted against it, there be no road between. This is a sharp time, now, a precise time—we live no longer in the dusky afternoon when evil mixed itself with good and befuddled the world. Now, by God's grace, the shining sun is up, and them that fear not light will surely praise it." —Judge Danforth presiding over the Salem witch-trials (Arthur Miller, *The Crucible*, Act III)

A funny thing happened on the way to the Leveson Inquiry. What began as a response to past cases of phone-hacking involving one private detective working for a closed newspaper became an extraordinary judicial inquisition into the entire "culture and ethics" of the British media. Then the Leveson Inquiry expanded into something even more extraordinary—an inquisition into almost all of the cultural and ethical ills of our society, apparently empowered to banish evil everywhere from parliament to the police force, and to right wrongs ranging from corruption in government circles to pornography in the local newsagents.

We were faced with an almost medieval spectacle of a judge and his top lawyer acting as priestly men of wisdom, apparently drawing their authority from some higher power, to interrogate and pass judgement on elected politicians and other public figures from the mortal world. That might have seemed strange and worrying enough. Stranger and more worrying still, however, was that so many rational and liberal-minded figures chose not merely to kowtow to the unreasonable power of the inquisition, but to cheer on the legal inquisitors and beg them to bring more wrong-doers to book.

Opening his inquiry into the British press in November 2011, Lord Justice Leveson (Liverpool College and Merton College, Oxford) went back to his classics to pose the "simple question" he said was at the heart of the issue: "Who guards the guardians?" By which he presumably meant, while the press is keeping an eye on public life, who polices the press?

There are other questions that should have been central to the Leveson Inquiry. For instance: who judges the judges? What business might it be of the unelected, unaccountable Lord Justice Leveson, assisted by a Queen's Counsel and a hand-picked panel of experts, to decide how far we might turn back the clock on the historic fight for press freedom? Why should judges and lawyers define what sort of reporting is in the "public interest" in a society where the public is at liberty to choose for itself? In short: who made m'lud and m'learned friends the "guardian" (takes out thesaurus: baby-sitter, chaperone, cop, supervisor, warden...) of freedom of expression?

Nobody asked any such questions. While Lord Justice Leveson and his legal counsel, Robert Jay QC, demanded answers from prime ministers and leading politicians, media editors and proprietors, top celebrities and Piers Morgan, none of the great and (sometimes not-so-)good saw fit to question their right to do so. The most extraordinary thing about the entire extraordinary Inquiry was the extent of the acquiescence to its authority and mission.

Almost the first time somebody sent a tricky question back to Lord Justice Leveson was six months into the Inquiry, in May 2012, when Michael Gove, the Conservative secretary of state for education, was summoned late in the game to explain some remarks he had made to reporters, warning that the Inquiry could have a "chilling effect" on press freedom. The good Lord Justice did not like that. Leveson liked even less Gove's insistence on the primacy of freedom of expression over the need for regulation, and his point that "by definition, free speech doesn't mean anything unless some people are going to be offended some of the time".[1]

When Leveson suggested that publications which refused to sign up to his new system of regulation could be hit with higher costs, the minister suggested that meant "the law would punish those who chose not to enter a voluntary method of regulation". No, no, insisted an irritated Leveson, all he meant was that those who refused to join a "sensible, approved system" would have to face the financial consequences. To which Gove responded, in his familiar dry style, "All I would say to that is — sensible to whom? Approved by whom?"

Yes, minister. Who is to say that standards which Lord Justice Leveson approves are the sensible ones for the public press? That was the sort of pertinent question that somebody might have raised about the standing of this entire Inquiry from the start—not least perhaps somebody from Gove's coalition government which set the thing up in the first place. Yet after six months of normally outspoken media people, politicians, lobbyists and campaigners appearing before the Leveson Inquiry, few had apparently thought to question its assumption of authority over the future of a free press.

It is hard to see why anybody with an ounce of feeling for freedom of expression should have endorsed the Leveson Inquiry. The genteel proceedings at the Royal Court of Justice were not a neutral talking shop, far less an agent for progressive change in the media. They represented an act of state intervention in the affairs of the press.

Called an inquiry, the Leveson business could be better understood as an inquisition. True, it was not an exercise in religious persecution (Lord Justice Leveson, himself an orthodox Jew, would make an unlikely Torquemada). Although several witnesses appeared pained by the experience, there was no physical torture involved, even of the "comfy chair" variety. Yet its mission, like other less civilised inquisitions before it, was to enforce a ruling orthodoxy, a dominant worldview to which all are expected to subscribe.

The goal of Leveson's well-mannered legal inquisitors has been much the same as their zealous religious forebears: to root out heretical views. In this case, to purge the popular press of the heresies which those in high places find distasteful and offensive. Behind the high-minded talk of ethics, this was a polite exercise in "ethical" cleansing, a disinfecting of the lower orders of the press. The mission of the inquisition was not censorship or book-burning, but to redefine press freedom by instilling an ethos of conformism across the media.

That would have been bad news enough. However, if there was to be a straight fight between the state regulators and the defenders of press freedom, bring it on. Far worse was that such a fight never started. There was no backlash against the Leveson Leviathan. Far from rushing to the barricades, many of those who are meant to champion free speech and civil liberties rushed down to the Royal Courts of Justice to wait their turn to be interrogated. Some apparently begged for the opportunity to be given a stiff going over by Mr Jay in front of the rolling TV news cameras, while many others cheered Leveson and Jay on from the media and Twitter sidelines.

Of course it has always been hard to take a public stand against a powerful inquisition. A combination of fear, power-lessness and cowardice stymied opposition to the Spanish Inquisition from the fifteenth century, the Salem witch-trials of 1692, and the McCarthyite anti-communist witch-hunts of the 1940s and 1950s. During the era of McCarthyism in the USA, even the Supreme Court refused to uphold the First Amendment rights of the blacklisted "Hollywood Ten". Only a few brave individuals have ever been able to maintain a principled stand when put under direct inquisitorial pressure.

Something very different has been happening around the latest inquisition, however. In the lines quoted above from Arthur Miller's 1952 play, *The Crucible*, which was set in Salem but dealt with the contemporary issues around McCarthyism in America, the authoritarian Judge Danforth issues an ominous warning that everybody must now openly side with the witch-hunt, or be deemed to be against it and on the side of evil. Sixty years later in London, Lord Justice Leveson had no need to make such a with-us-or-against-us threat, even if he had been so inclined. Almost nobody was against his "court" in the first place.

People buckled under to the Leveson Inquiry's authority and the orthodoxy it preached without any threat of torture, death, imprisonment, blacklisting or being sent to bed with no supper. Something other than fear was at work here. What we witnessed in response to Leveson was less a mass outbreak of cowardice than a general attitude of willing collusion. Tabloid-hating journalists and campaigners who consider themselves of a liberal persuasion voluntarily signed up to the confederacy for conformism, and became cheerleaders for the "ethical" clean-sers. It seems as if many have internalised the inquisition's worldview.

This is the biggest danger to a free press and freedom of expression posed by the Leveson Inquiry. It would not much matter which particular system of press regulation it finally proposed (Leveson's report has not been published at the time of writing), or whether the government endorsed it. What matters more is that it has already consolidated broad support for the purging of the press and the spirit of conformism.

Zimbabwe-on-Sea?

Such has been the degree of confusion about the role of the Leveson Inquiry that it seems as well to restate some basic points that should have been obvious. For a start, that the Leveson Inquiry was not a "great opportunity" or a neutral forum to discuss different forms of press regulation and the limits of state intervention in the media. The Leveson Inquiry itself WAS a political act of state intervention in the press, of a sort unseen in the UK in modern times.

Those who claim that the Leveson Inquiry has been about seeking justice on behalf of "all our society" will point out that everybody involved, not least the Lord Justice himself, made clear that they were against political interference in the media. This misses the point. We should judge people and institutions by what they do, not what they say about themselves.

The Inquiry was announced in parliament by the prime minister of the United Kingdom, David Cameron, not simply to look into the phone-hacking scandal but to examine the entire culture and ethics of the media. It had the full support of Her Majesty's Opposition. It has been headed by a senior judge, Lord Justice Brian Leveson. It sat in the Royal Courts of Justice, taking evidence under oath. The prime minister made clear at the start that he would seek to implement whatever system of press regulation Leveson proposed, even in the unlikely event that he came up with a plan for full state regulation. (The government has since seemed to want to qualify that commitment.)

A body set up and bankrolled by Her Majesty's Government, fronted by a leading law officer of the Crown, deploying the considerable resources of the judicial machinery and with the power of the legislature behind it to shape the future scope of press regulation is no "independent" talking shop. The Leveson Inquiry has been a politico-judicial intervention in the affairs of a free press, by any other name.

It might come as a shock to some, but state interference in the press need not mean politicians dictating what newspapers write in their editorials. Judges and officials are central components of the state machinery. Ask Lord Justice Leveson. Discussing the need to regulate content on the web as well as in print, he talked about creating a process "which the State, and I don't mean government, has an interest in seeing is conducted on a level playing field".[2] That let the official cat out of the bag. The state is far more than the elected government of the day. It is the administrative, judicial and armed machine that rules society and protects the status quo. Having judges and official ombudsmen intervene in the press is just as much state interference as politicians poking their noses in. It is arguably worse. At least we can get rid of politicians if we don't like what they do. Judges and officials are unaccountable state agents beyond our recall. Those seeking the modern incarnation of growing "power without responsibility", the accusation hurled at press barons, might look no further than the judicial bench.

But, protest those who appear more concerned to defend Leveson than stand up for press freedom, the likes of me are just scaremongering about state censorship, by making out that any attempt to regulate the press will turn the UK into Zimbabwe! In fact I am aware that we do not live in Zimbabwe. For a start that blighted African state is one of the few countries on earth with even worse libel laws than those we labour under, which can get journalists arrested and jailed for criminal libel (a practice that the British taught their colonial subjects in the good old days), rather than simply silenced and bankrupted in the civilised British style.

If we are concerned about laws infringing press freedom — and we should be — there is no need for horror-fantasy scenarios about Leveson turning the UK into Zimbabwe-on-Sea. From the Official Secrets Act downwards there is already no shortage of respectable British laws that hem in the freedom of the press. Fifteen years ago one study put the count of such laws at around 50 and rising. Since then a wave of new statutes against "hate speech", plus a plethora of laws ranging from the Regulation of Investigatory Powers Act 2000 to the Bribery Act 2010, have added to the roll-call of legislative shame.

The biggest monsters are the UK's libel laws, challengers to be named the worst acts on the British statute books (a title won in the face of some pretty stiff competition). These defamation laws have not only made the courts of London the favoured holiday destination of rich and powerful "libel tourists" from around the world, who will travel the globe to ask British judges to suppress and punish their critics. More importantly the libel laws have had a "chilling effect" on the UK media, institutionalising timidity and a fear of publishing the controversial even if you believe it to be true.

This is an issue on which I am unfortunately something of an expert, having been sued for libel by a major media corporation and its journalists. I lost, as libel defendants tend to do, with the result that *LM*, the independent magazine of which I was editor was bankrupted and forced to close down, and my publisher and I were left with a personal bill of around a million quid in costs and damages. As I said to the press pack after the trial in March 2000, on the steps of the same Royal Courts of Justice where Lord Justice Leveson sat in judgement on press freedom, "the only thing this case has proved beyond reasonable doubt is that the libel laws are a menace to a free press and a disgrace to democracy".[3]

Now there are moves afoot to reform the libel laws, with the coalition government apparently listening to the reform lobby. The proposed modest changes look too much like tinkering around the edges, designed to offer some protection to "responsible" scientists and academics, and will leave the central threat of the libel law to a free press intact. Indeed by limiting access to jury trials in future, the new proposals might only increase the power of judges to decide what is fit for us to write and read. Yet the proposals have been excitedly welcomed by respectable civil liberties campaigners. What about freedom for those writers whom the judges consider "irresponsible"?

The point here is that there is already no shortage of legal impediments to a free press to protest about—and no need to pretend that Lord Justice Leveson is some whited-up version of Robert Mugabe, intent on imposing more. Because outright state censorship was never the issue at stake in the debate around the Leveson Inquiry. We are not facing the "Orwellian nightmare" of *1984*-style repression, governments editing newspapers and jackboots stamping on journalists' faces forever. That would at least be straightforward enough to oppose. The threat today is more insidious.

"Ethical" Cleansing

If some sensitive souls object to the Inquiry being called an inquisition, how about "show trial"? The popular media has certainly been on trial for its freedom and its future, and the proceedings surely met the historical standard of a trial "held for show, the guilt of the accused person having been decided in advance"; a trial "conducted primarily to make a particular impression on the public". The verdict has been clear from before Lord Justice Leveson sat down. The popular press has been found guilty and only the precise details of the sentence remained to be decided. It was always fairly unlikely that Leveson would recommend that anybody be taken out and shot. Nonetheless the show trial of the tabloids has been conducted "to make a particular impression on the public".

From the start, the Leveson Inquiry was at pains to draw a line between the culture and practice of the ethical press and the rest. And what is wrong with that, you might ask? Who wants to support an "unethical" press, any more than they wish to endorse "unsustainable development" in the economy?

The trouble is, as discussed earlier, ethics are not as clear or straightforward as some would have them appear. Ethical codes in any area of public life, and perhaps especially the press, do not descend from the ether. What are presented as timeless, universal ethical values are in reality an expression of particular interests and outlooks in specific historical circumstances (see chapter two). The high-minded language of ethics is often a code for expressing more down-to-earth interests. Religious zealots might call on the omnipotent authority of their God in support of their personal prejudices; zealous secular crusaders can invoke the holy name of ethereal "ethics" to endorse their own earthbound agenda.

Today, authorities and experts who lack the courage or conviction to express their aims explicitly will instead seek to smuggle them into effect behind the seductive banner of "ethical practice". The ethical option tends to be whatever you want to happen, particularly if it involves policing the actions of others. Ethics thus becomes a way of laying down the law on what is and is not acceptable to those who write the code. The rest of us are free to conform to their "ethical" diktat.

In the case of the Leveson Inquiry and the storm of opinion surrounding it, the emphasis on ethics has served as a justific-ation for promoting the "ethical" cleansing of the press: for separating the respectable journalism of which Leveson and his supporters approve, from the disreputable "popular" rabble beneath. Leveson's cohorts have deployed the notion of "ethical journalism" as a banner behind which to push a narrow conventional view of the world and how it should be reported.

Robert Jay, the QC acting as counsel to the Inquiry, laid out in his opening statement that they would not confine their investigation to phone-hacking but would also examine any other "illegal and unethical" practices used to obtain stories, from subterfuge to blagging. Yet these are all the tools of investigative journalism, used by reporters who often have to sail close to the wind to uncover truths that somebody does not want to see revealed. Underhand methods, possibly including rooting through somebody's bins or even voicemails, have often been the only way for journalists to get answers others would rather not give.

However, the Inquiry's top lawyer was at pains to insist that they were not opposed to investigative journalism as such. What examples did Jay give of investigations of which Leveson and co might approve? It came as no great surprise that he cited the *Guardian's* crusade over *News of the World* phone-hacking, and the *Daily Telegraph's* revelations about MPs' expenses. The first of these campaigns relied on publishing information from police sources, strictly accurate or otherwise, while the other involved printing documents handed over by an informant. The irony is that until July 2011, one British paper which had still been investing serious resources in making and breaking investigative news stories using underhand methods was the tabloid *News of the World*, notably through its brilliant "fake sheikh" set-ups. But those distasteful probings did not meet with the legal establishment's approval.

A similar double standard masquerading as ethics was evident in the Leveson Inquiry's attitude to what some witnesses described as "salacious gossip" or tabloid "tittle-tattle". That is, celebrity gossip as reported by the popular press, you understand. Not to be confused with the important revelations coaxed out at the Inquiry about the PM mistakenly texting "LOL" to Rebekah Brooks, which had the lawyers and liberal pundits salivating and LOL. A case of our gossip is ethically superior to yours. "This is such fun!" the lead counsel Robert Jay QC reportedly "mouthed to a colleague" as Leveson broke for lunch during his cross-examination of James Murdoch, apparently wallowing in the he-said-she-said mire just as much as any lunchtime TV panellist.[4]

The panel chosen to sit behind Lord Justice Leveson during his inquiry into the press—the hand-picked jury in this trial—gave a flavour of whose ethics might be encoded there. Alongside Sir David Bell, former chairman of the house journal of UK capitalism, the *Financial Times*, sat Lord Currie, a former director of the broadcasting regulator, Ofcom. The journalism profession was represented by Elinor Goodman, former political editor of the liberal middle classes' flagship *Channel 4 News*, and George Jones, former political editor of the conservative middle classes' newspaper the *Daily Telegraph*. Then there was Sir Paul Scott-Lee, the former Chief Constable of West Midlands Police, a post not always immediately associated with the sterling defence of press freedom. And lastly Shami Chakrabarti, director of Liberty (formerly the National Council for Civil Liberties), the sort of selective civil rights campaigner who supports restrictions on free speech for those whose views she deems unacceptable. Little wonder if tabloid journalists felt they were not exactly being tried before a jury of their peers.

The effect of this exercise in "ethical" cleansing was to draw a line in the sand, to say that the freedom of the press extends to this point "but..." no further. Any tabloid journalist or editor that sees fit to cross into territory beyond the proscribed borders of ethical correctness will risk losing their legitimacy; some would have them lose their licence to write and publish altogether.

If you can draw such a line and create a chilling climate of conformism, then who needs censorship? There has always been a strong streak of self-censorship in the British press, which has generally made formal censorship as unnecessary as it would be awkward for Britain's reputation. George Orwell nailed this back in 1945, in a short essay on "The Freedom of the

Press" that he originally wrote as a preface to *Animal Farm*, his satire on a post-revolutionary totalitarian state based on Stalin's Soviet Union (ironically the publisher did not see fit to include the preface about free speech in the first edition of *Animal Farm*, and most publishers of subsequent editions have followed suit).

In "The Freedom of the Press", Orwell noted that, even during the crisis years of the Second World War, state censorship in Britain had not been "particularly irksome". There had been no need for it, since the press had generally censored itself. "Unpopular ideas can be silenced, and inconvenient facts kept dark, without the need for any official ban… [T]hings which on their own merits would get the big headlines [have been] kept right out of the British press, not because the Government intervened but because of a general tacit agreement that 'it wouldn't do' to mention that particular fact."

This sort of "veiled censorship", Orwell observed, operated not only in the popular press but also across the cultural spectrum in books, magazines, plays, movies and radio. The key thing was the creation of "an orthodoxy, a body of ideas which it is assumed that all right-thinking people will accept without question. It is not exactly forbidden to say this, that or the other, but it is 'not done' to say it, just as in mid-Victorian times it was 'not done' to mention trousers in the presence of a lady. Anyone who challenges the prevailing orthodoxy finds himself silenced with surprising effectiveness. A genuinely unfashionable opinion is almost never given a fair hearing, either in the popular press or in the highbrow periodicals".[5]

Orwell was referring in particular to the informal agreement across the British press and beyond that it "wouldn't do" to criticise Stalin's repressive regime while the Soviets were Britain's allies in the Second World War. Today the political-media elite is seeking to consolidate a new "orthodoxy" which "it is assumed all right-thinking people will accept without question". They are fighting a culture war to cleanse the popular press and those who consume it of things that "wouldn't do". No state censorship required if conformism rules.

Robert the Apostle?

As I say, the Leveson Inquiry began as a remarkable inquisition into the press. Then it transmogrified into something even more extraordinary—an inquisition into all the ills of society. The ever-expanding remit of Leveson confirmed the central role of the press in public life today; once an inquiry is about the media, it becomes all-consuming.

The most revealing figure in this was that of Robert Jay QC, Leveson's lead legal counsel. A borderline unctuous figure, Jay appeared to have adopted an almost Apostolic role as a man on a mission, the seeker of truth, the grand inquisitor. He was praised in legal circles as the ideal lawyer for such a "non-partisan" role. In his questioning of witnesses, especially those connected with the Murdoch and tabloid press, Jay appeared non-partisan only in the sense of acting like a figure from a higher moral plane, floating above the grubby fray and peering down with disdain at those beneath both his nose and his contempt. He even lectured them about their poor use of the English language whilst showing off his own dictionary-swallowing skills in making "pellucidly clear" points, highlighting "nugatory" arguments and examining the "propinquity" of politicians.[6] By the end some might have thought Jay's "ethical" prejudices were, to borrow the phrase he used against Rebekah Brooks, "as plain as a pikestaff".

Yet rather than criticise or lampoon Jay's inflated status, many observers praised and encouraged it. The good Lord Justice Leveson and his apostle Robert were depicted as fighting the noble fight to save the press if not the whole political system, and possibly the entire planet. Instead of questioning where the rattling train of an inquiry was heading, commentators and campaigners rushed to get their own pet hates about the press and politics added on to the Inquiry's endlessly elastic agenda.

It was another reflection of how central the media has become to public life that an inquiry into the press should be widely seen as an opportunity to sort out all the perceived ills of our society. Many lobbyists seemed to look upon Leveson and

Jay as a sympathetic alternative to the type of democratic political debate that proves so resistant to their causes. How much
easier to persuade these well-schooled, quietly spoken gents
than the rough-house mob in the world outside the courts! The
Lord Justice and the QC were turned into political fantasy figures, a sort of two-man "UK Spring" by those desperate for
some ethical-legal short-cut to their chosen goal. A few months
into the Inquiry one radical outlet was even selling Lord Justice
Leveson t-shirts, featuring an image of their hero—the "cult, no-
nonsense figure cutting a swathe through the seedy relationship
between the media, politicians and the police"—in judge's wig,
with the legend *Taking Care of Business*.

Before long, different lobby groups were appealing to
Leveson to sort out issues to do with privacy law, ownership of
the press, Page 3 pin-ups and political sleaze, alongside changing the entire culture of the national media, banishing a hated
press baron from our shores and possibly bringing down a
cabinet minister or even the entire coalition government.

We were confronted by the frankly depressing spectacle of
civil liberties lobbyists and radical feminists appealing to a pillar
of the legal establishment to fight their battles for them, holding
out their begging bowls and pleading, "Please sir, can we have
some more rights?" As the political and media lobbyists loaded
greater and greater importance and hope onto the Inquiry,
imagining it as a substitute for politics, one dedicated Labour-
and-Leveson supporting columnist declared that "The Leveson
inquiry isn't about criminality, or one minister, or even one
proprietor: it's really about what kind of democracy we still
have".[7] Of course it is; so far as democracy is concerned, who
needs messy elections when you can have a nice neat judge-led
inquiry?

Changing Their Rules on Slebs and Victims

The overwhelmingly positive view of the Leveson Inquiry, even
within media circles and among those campaigning for free
speech, has been a stark illustration of the problem. It confirms
the consolidation of an orthodoxy, a single view that all must

subscribe to—in this case, that the popular media needs to be purged, first by a judge and then a powerful new regulator. The conformist orthodoxy created around Leveson represents perhaps the biggest "But…" of all about press freedom today.

One symptom has been the way that serious liberal journalists who pride themselves on their standards seem to have abandoned their normal rules of conduct in their eagerness to sign up to the Leveson mission.

Take for example the rule of Serious Liberal Journalism that declares: "All serious liberal journalists must totally despise celebrity culture and the obsession with the private lives of 'personalities'." We now have an amendment/exception to that rule: "EXCEPT when said celebrities do a star turn talking about their private lives in order to attack the tabloids and demand more press regulation at the Leveson Inquiry into the 'culture and ethics' of the UK media. Then they become heroes and the star-struck serious liberal media will start acting as celebrity cheerleaders."

Or the other rule of Serious Liberal Journalism which says that: "All serious liberal journalists will respect the victim-centred media culture. They will never criticise a high-profile victim or their relatives, but shall treat their views as sacrosanct at all times—see for example Stephen Lawrence's parents or the Hillsborough families." Now we have an amendment/exception to that rule too: "EXCEPT when the father of a victim of the 7/7 London bombings, whose phone was hacked, says that the Leveson Inquiry has been turned into a 'celebrity circus' to attack press freedom. In such circumstances serious journalists and liberal pundits shall rally to the celebrity crusaders' side and effectively tell the victim's father he doesn't know what he is on about."

In the strange goings-on around the various legal and parliamentary inquiries into press regulation in 2011–12, we witnessed the rehabilitation of celebrity culture in the eyes of the usually contemptuous liberal media. Campaigners for press regulation signed up to the fan club of those we might call Celebrities for Censorship. Hugh Grant was encouraged to strut around political and media circles in the guise of the right-on prime minister he played in the film *Love, Actually*, turning up at the Liberal Democrat conference to praise the *Guardian* as the "goodies" against the tabloid baddies. Steve Coogan, displaying the sort of inflated ego even his Alan Partridge character might find a bit much, was appointed spokesman for piety and "ordinary people", in which capacity he wrote the foreword for the *Guardian*'s Christmas annual, commanding us to "Make sure you are on the right side of the debate. The *Guardian* is".[8]

As they toured the inquiries into the media protesting live on TV about the invasion of their privacy, the showbiz tabloid-bashers were treated not only with respect but admiration and affection. Even their maddest-sounding allegations about the tabloid press having supposedly bugged them, burgled them and effectively hidden under their beds were reported as facts, despite the actual fact that, as Leveson's QC pointed out, there had been "plenty of them [allegations] with very little in the way of evidence". But what's an absence of evidence among friends? The Members of Parliament on the committee looking into injunctions and privacy referred to the three celebrities as "Hugh", "Steve" and "Max" [Mosley], barely holding back from asking their star guests for autographs and mobile phone photos. Meanwhile, the serious media reported Coogan's claims to be "speaking on behalf of ordinary people" against the tabloids as if they were the words of an elected statesman.

It was left to one of those "ordinary people" – Graham Foulkes, whose phone was allegedly hacked after his son was killed in the 7/7 terror attacks – to put the slebs in their place. He told *The Times* that he would not want to appear before the judge-led Inquiry, which had been "hijacked" by celebrities "for their own purposes". "Leveson was set up around phone hacking," said Mr Foulkes, "but it has become a celebrity circus. Those same celebrities who have ensured they're in the press all the time, and now they're crying foul. It's completely wrong." Mr Foulkes expressed "great concerns" that the Inquiry would end in "kneejerk" legislation to leave newspapers controlled by politicians with a grudge against them.[9]

In response, Coogan puffed himself up even further and told BBC Radio 4's *Today* programme that, far from having "hijacked" the Leveson Inquiry, celebrities such as him were doing a public service by acting as "the mouthpiece" for ordinary people—even if, like Graham Foulkes, those people could clearly speak for themselves.[10] More remarkable than this self-regarding response was the reaction of the serious liberal press, normally so contemptuous of all things sleb. Instead of laughing Coogan and co out of the High Court, they rallied to the celebrity crusaders' banners and defended Leveson against Graham Foulkes.

One leading columnist, who has been hailed as a "freedom fighter" and a "hero" of the struggle for for civil liberties, weighed in heavily on the side of the judicial inquisition against the press, declaring that Leveson "is for all of our society, not just celebrities". Our hero not only bravely compared the British tabloids to the Russian secret police (stopping short of multi-millionaire Tory MP Zac Goldsmith's comparison of the tabloids with Auschwitz), but even concluded that "freedom of expression has been actually increased rather than jeopardised by the Inquiry".[11]

It is right to say that the Leveson Inquiry was not just about celebrities. It has been about sanitising the British press and regulating the tastes of its "ordinary" readers. It is also right to say that the likes of Coogan and Grant are acting as "mouthpieces". Not, however, for justice or the common people. They are being used as willing mouthpieces for those who despise the "popular" press—and, more importantly, its mass readership—and would rather see press freedom reserved for the "goodies" practising "proper public-interest journalism", as defined by right-on editors and judges.

The true attitude of the Inquiry towards the views of those "ordinary people" that everybody kept waxing lyrical about was rather better illustrated by an exchange quite early in proceedings between Lord Justice Leveson and Ian Hislop, the editor of *Private Eye*. Insisting that "I believe in a free press and I don't believe in a regulated press", Hislop said instead that the press should be held to account by existing criminal law, and beyond that by "the people who buy the papers". Then he made a suggestion that shook the legal elitists present. "I do hope", said Hislop, "you're going to call some members of the public and ask them why they bought the *News of the World*, what they thought they were getting." Allow members of the public to address a public inquiry? Have *News of the World* readers holding forth at hearings about that newspaper? Risk having them say that they loved its attitude and missed their familiar portion of Sunday sauce? The very idea! "I don't think", retorted Lord Justice Leveson, "we'll necessarily do it in quite that way." No, not quite. Or in fact, not at all.[12]

So yes, it is also right to say that people need to decide which side they are on in this battle. But it was never a straight fight between the press barons and people, as Coogan claims. There has been far more than the Murdoch empire in the dock here. The principles of a free press are under judicial and political assault. The battle lines are being drawn between those who wholeheartedly support press freedom, and the many more who claim they support it, "But..." There can rarely have been a more one-sided battle, with so many deserting to the inquisitors' camp.

It is difficult to believe that battle-hardened figures in the media could really be naïve enough to imagine that a more closely regulated media would only affect the "baddies" in the tabloids. Perhaps they are simply pompous enough to believe that the world really would be a better place if their sort of goodie had a monopoly on what could be written and read by others. Either way, it looks as if they are on the wrong side.

Self-Regulation "Tougher than the Police"?

A sure sign of the conformism created around the Leveson Inquiry is that almost all influential parties to the discussion agree on the need for tougher press regulation. Historical cases of criminal phone-hacking linked to one private detective, which should be left to the police, have become accepted as the pretext for a purge of the UK press. This consensus means it did not much matter which particular proposals for reform the Leveson Inquiry finally put forward, or whether the government endorsed them. The important thing was that, publicly at least, almost everybody accepted the need for more control and a more narrow definition of what is acceptable or "ethical" in journalism.

What has the debate about different forms of regulation really been about? Nobody who is taken seriously favours full-on state regulation of the press. On the other hand all of them effectively endorse the fallacy that the UK press has been too free.

Lord Justice Leveson, his celebrity chorus and the coalition government indicated throughout that they were inclined towards some form of tough new "independent" watchdog to reform the press, but with a "statutory backdrop" or "statutory back-up". That is, a law to give the new watchdog muscle, in particular to press all newspapers to sign up to the regulatory body, possibly with some financial penalties for dissenters — which sounds like an indirect form of state licensing of the press.

How did the media critics of political interference respond to these ideas? A few tried to hold the line; James Harding, editor of *The Times*, told Leveson that if the authorities sought effectively to compel the press to comply with any new regulatory system, "then you have a system of licensing of newspapers".[13] But many more broadly accepted, even embraced, Leveson's approach. The *Guardian* acknowledged that "The British press is arguably under-regulated and over-legislated".[14] Well, half-right anyway. But under-regulated? Perhaps they feel the need for more guidance in editing the *Guardian*. Or like middle class childcare experts who demand compulsory parenting classes, is it only those other, irresponsible parents and newspapers they are talking about?

In response to the proposals for statutory-backed regulation, the rump of the old regime appeared to offer a defence of the self-regulation of the press. Yet what they were really proposing appeared little different to the hardline pro-regulation lobby.

Lord Hunt, head of the old Press Complaints Commission, first responded to Leveson by formally abolishing the PCC—a gesture of submission to the new order. Then Hunt announced that the problem with the PCC was it had never really been a regulator—that is, it had lacked the power to enforce its rules on the press. He declared that he would come up with a new "self-regulation" body with teeth. What this lawyer and former Tory cabinet minister had in mind soon became clear. Under head-lines such as "Press watchdog could have more powers than police", it was reported that Hunt wanted all newspapers to sign binding legal contracts that would give his new body "absolute discretion" to raid newspaper offices, seize docu-ments and emails, question journalists in taped interviews and impose huge fines—without the right to appeal—on anybody deemed to have breached the new rules. Such sweeping powers might be available to police states elsewhere, but not currently to the British police. So much for the "alternative" on offer as regards self-regulation and a free press.[15]

There have also been several proposals from within the media about treating journalism as more of a "proper profess-ion" that can easily be cleaned up. Experts and academics have suggested that journalism should be self-regulated along similar lines to the legal or medical professions, with the implication that a disciplinary body could punish those who don't come up to the required standard or even have them "struck off". Some have spelt out this approach by reviving the old proposals for journalists to be licensed—as they once had to be by the King's censors (see chapter three). Paul Dacre of the *Mail* newspapers, a doughty defender of the tabloid press, suggested to the Leveson Inquiry that the press could create a register of accred-ited journalists, make it tougher to get an official press card—and remove accreditation from miscreants. "It will be the news-paper industry registering and disciplining journalists, not the state", Dacre told Leveson.[16] His ideas were endorsed by the broadsheet *Independent*. Who needs the state to discipline the press, when it appears willing to self-flagellate?

Indeed the *Independent* appeared to have nailed its colours to the licensing mast even before the Leveson Inquiry properly set sail. In September 2011 the Labour Party's culture spokesman, Ivan Lewis, in the grip of an apparent spasm of illiberalism, suddenly suggested at the party conference that journalists guilty of "gross malpractice" could be "struck off" and prevented from publishing. Labour leader Ed Miliband quickly announced that a journalists' register was not party policy (yet). But the new editor of the *Independent*, Chris Blackhurst, rallied to defend Lewis's idea on BBC radio: "I know there's an issue with the fact that there is a register of journalists, but frankly maybe we should", he said. "There ought to be an ability to have that person removed. Let's not just look at doctors, all sorts of professions... The Jockey Club. They actually bar jockeys from riding horses. Why can't we bar journalists from writing articles?"[17]

It is important to encourage journalism of a professional standard, in terms of being serious, honest and rational. That, however, is very different from turning journalism into a closed profession, like the law or medicine, which you cannot enter without the required qualifications and from which you can be debarred for breaking the rules or breaching the etiquette handed down from above. Journalism is nothing more than the paid—and increasingly these days, the unpaid—exercise of the general right to freedom of expression. It should be treated as an open calling, not a closed profession which polices its entrants either by social class or "ethical" standing. The emerging support for some form of licensing or professional accreditation confirms the growing acceptance of a need to narrow the scope of journalism and the press.

It has effectively been assumed without question on all sides that firmer regulation is necessary. However much those concerned may protest otherwise, that is another way of saying that the press is too free. You do not pass more stringent rules and laws (sorry, statutory back-ups) in order to liberate the press or widen free speech.

Who Wants to Live in Hugh's "Ideal World"?

In the run-up to the Leveson Inquiry supporters of the purging of the press got so carried away that they demanded firmer police action against errant newspapers and journalists. When the Met took their advice and started arresting hacks in dawn raids, some of these people became a little queasy. The alarm grew when the Metropolitan Police briefly threatened to prosecute the *Guardian* over the leaking of details of the phone-hacking investigation in 2011. Why are you picking on us, liberal lawyers and journalists protested to the Met, we're on the same side in this!

This touching display of faith in the progressive ethics of PC Plod seemed a tad unworldly. Yet in a sense they were right – the Metropolitan Police and the liberal media have indeed been on the same side in the battle to purge the press and enforce the new conformism. This was clear even in the Met's initial statement attempting to justify its threat, where the force stated that "We pay tribute to the *Guardian*'s unwavering determination to expose the hacking scandal and their challenge around the initial police response. We also recognise the important public interest of whistleblowing and investigative reporting". With the Met sounding as if they were giving the *Guardian* an award rather than a summons, it came as little surprise when the police dropped the case soon after that, announcing that "We do not want to interfere with journalists".[18]

In fact the Met now appears dedicated to interfering with journalists, against whom it has mounted the biggest operation in British criminal history over phone-hacking and allegations of improper payments. It's just that it only has the nerve to interfere with journalists from what are seen as the wrong side of the ethical tracks, enforcing the Leveson line. And while the liberal media were cock-a-hoop over their success in turning the police away from the *Guardian*'s door, most remained content enough for it to be open season on the *Sun* and its reporters. This display of double-standards confirmed the danger press freedom is in today.

Suppose that those allegedly liberal media campaigners got their way, and the authorities restricted themselves to only "interfering" with the tabloid press, while leaving alone those who conformed to the new rules on behaving like "goodies". What sort of a victory for a free press or a democratic society would that be, to find ourselves living under a one-party (the Supper Party?) state of non-jackbooted intolerant values?

Once again it was left to Hugh Grant to spell out these matters. In March 2012 he appeared on BBC 2's *Newsnight* programme to rebut Lord Hunt's proposals for continued self-regulation of the press (the actor had been invited to meet with Hunt, reflecting his elevated status as voice-over artist for the "press freedom, But..." lobby). *Newsnight* presenter Jeremy Paxman at least maintained a rare note of cynicism about Grant's new standing, introducing him as "the press spokesman for Hacked Off", the campaign set up in response to the phone-hacking scandal, and describing Grant as a world-famous actor "best known for his appearances on *Newsnight*".[19]

Lord Hunt, Hugh told Jeremy, is "a great defender of the freedom of the press and quite rightly so. But"—there is always a But—"I and my fellow campaigners and the victims we represent" see things differently. Having nobly assumed the role, unelected and unrewarded, as representative of victims everywhere, Grant insisted that Lord Hunt's idea of voluntary contracts would not work and that he had this on good authority from "my legal friends who know more about this than I do". Which rather begged the question as to why they were not appearing in the media instead of him, but then lawyers don't generally turn journalists weak at the knees.

In the middle of these exchanges, during which Grant decided off the cuff that yes, probably Twitter should be regulated too, he delivered perhaps his most telling remark of all: "And no one, listen, in an ideal world of course the press should be self-regulating. It's only by looking at history and the repeated failure of that to happen that regrettably it's come to this." In Hugh Grant's "ideal world", perhaps Notting Hill booksellers really could get off with Julia Roberts, Britain really might have a dashing, dancing prime minister who tells off those dreadful Yanks and believes in Love, Actually, and all newspapers would be "goodies" pursuing high-minded ethical journalism rather than celebrity gossip, about, say, such trifles as a famous actor enjoying the company of a sex industry worker on a public highway. So long as they conformed to that "ideal", the press might be left to regulate itself.

But of course we do not live in Grant's or anybody else's ideal world. In the real world, the exercise of liberty is a sticky business and always has been. Not everybody who chooses to use the freedom of the press will have the moral standards or the piety of a celebrity crusader. That is no excuse for impinging on that fundamental freedom or forcing others to comply with what Grant called "your code of ethics". Whose code might that be, then? Talk about transcendental "ethical codes" is always itself a code for pursuing particular interests and agendas – in this case, the demand for restricting freedom of expression.

Could anything be worse than being forced to live in Grant's sanitised "ideal world"? He even suggested that "looking at history" shows the need for state-backed regulation. Perhaps he has studied some different history from me, but my reading suggests that British history has been one long struggle to free the press from legal restraints, licensing, taxation and other means of state control, now apparently to be casually, though "regrettably" tossed aside.

At another, calmer moment the views of actors on press freedom and regulation might not carry quite so much weight in serious circles. However, in the current surreal atmosphere the likes of Grant have become celebrity voice-over artists for a powerful lobby to purge the popular press. Of course, they say, we don't really want to see tabloid newspapers closed down and journalists arrested. We just want them all to be "perfect".

In February 2012 Charlie Brooker, shouty television presenter and TV critic, indulged in a 120-second rhyming rant against the *Sun* on Channel 4, sounding like an allegedly liberal journalist's version of *Big Brother*'s two-minute hate. Yet days later, as the *Sun on Sunday* was launched, Brooker wrote to express the pious hope that the expanding tabloid might now use its new dawn to "reinvent" itself. Brooker assured his readers that he believes in "reform, not capital punishment'" for sinners such as the *Sun*, since "only a monopolist wants to shut the other side up". In this spirit, the critic advised the *Sun* that it "needs to rehabilitate itself", become less "bullying" and more "fun", in a strictly ethical way. Thus in order to pass the Brooker test of proper fun newspapers the *Sun* will have to get rid of Page 3 and its "pointless helping of naked breasts". It seemed that the *Sun on Sunday* could be tolerated, just so long as it agreed to turn itself into something that would not offend the Sabbath sensibilities of more decent folk. For "reform", read conform. The monopolists of today do not want to "shut the other side up", but merely to redefine press freedom so that all read from their boring script. Verily, Charlie Brooker appears to want the *Sun* to shine out of his backside.[20]

You Can't Say THAT

The Leveson Inquiry and the responses to it have captured the spirit of the age—unfortunately. In its current mood of self-censorship and acquiescence to purging the popular press, the media is once again only reflecting and reinforcing cultural trends emanating from wider society. In this case, the powerful cultural message is You Can't Say THAT, which has become a staple of our increasingly narrow public and political debate.

In recent years we have experienced the creeping influence of two closely related strands of thought. The first of these ugly twins is an increasingly illiberal strain of liberalism, which sees more laws and regulations and bans as the way to force the masses to enjoy their human rights in a civilised fashion. The other stands for intolerance in the name of tolerance, which says that anything which transgresses the narrow parameters of right-on speech or thought must be outlawed.

Both of these strains reflect the political and cultural elites' loss of faith in humanity. No longer are people seen as robust and morally autonomous beings. Instead we are viewed as vulnerable and malleable in equal measure, in need of protection from "offensive" words and images that could either cause us pain or incite us to cause it to others.

The message that You Can't Say THAT has been used to try to limit or close down discussion on a range of controversial issues, from race and immigration to climate change or religion and sexuality. It began in the UK as a cultural mainstay of New Labour, but has since been embraced with enthusiasm by the Conservative-Lib Dem coalition. As London's Tory mayor Boris Johnson proudly declared in banning bus adverts from Christians who claimed to be able to "cure" homosexuality, we are now officially "intolerant of intolerance".

In the age of intolerant tolerance and illiberal liberalism, it often appears that to say something offensive is considered the worst offence of all. It would be hard to think of anything further removed from genuine tolerance. Since the idea emerged during the Enlightenment, tolerance has meant allowing others freely to express their ideas and opinions—even or especially those with which you might disagree. But being tolerant has never been a case of passively sitting back and taking it. It involves having all the arguments out in the open, engaging with the ideas of others, arguing your corner—and confronting uncertainty. In this way tolerance is a means, as Professor Frank Furedi puts it, for people to pursue their controversies and intellectual conflicts to "the bitter end", rather than closing down debates because somebody might say something offensive to somebody: "Criticism, and even disrespect of competing beliefs and views is entirely consistent with the act of tolerance … Society needs to regain the capacity to question, discriminate and judge."[21]

Or as Dr Samuel Johnson put it with typical bluntness, "Every man has the right to utter what he thinks truth—and every other man has the right to knock him down for it". Figuratively speaking, at the very least.[22]

Instead of that grown-up attitude what we have today is a culture of intolerant tolerance, where debate can be denied and words effectively outlawed in the name of avoiding offence. The punishment of our age for speaking out of turn is not normally to be censored pre-publication, but censured afterwards, with a heap of opprobrium—and possibly writs—coming down on the sinner's head from all directions, as a warning to all not to cross the line again.

More worrying yet, the only response appears to be, not a proper argument for freedom of expression, but rather infantile two-fingered gestures of political incorrectness as an end in themselves, as practised by cut-out characters such as a Jeremy Clarkson or a Russell Brand. That combination of intolerant tolerance and infantile tantrums sounds pretty close to the worst of all worlds.

The crusade for the "ethical" cleansing of the press is a product of this dark cultural shift that can only amplify the message of You Can't Say That. The internet offers us fresh opportunities to break out of this straitjacket. Current trends in the new media, however, suggest that those spaces are in danger of being not just wasted but turned into another no-go area for freedom of expression.

Who Needs Thought Police
When We Have the Twitter Taliban?

Twitter has become an internet phenomenon of recent years, both as an addition and an alternative to the mainstream media. This "real-time information network" where anybody can broadcast to a potential mass audience (albeit in just 140-character "tweets") has been hailed as big step forward for freedom of expression and the democratisation of debate. As Twitter's boss in the UK puts it, the social networking site sees itself as "the free speech wing of the free speech party".[23]

Sounds top. In practice, however, Twitter has also become home to some of the less wholesome trends in media debate today. So much so that it can sometimes look more like the intolerant wing of the intolerance party.

Any time somebody says something that strays outside the conformist orthodoxy today—especially in the mainstream media—they risk becoming the target of what has been called a Twitter mob, or a Twitch-hunt. Thousands of Twitter users will descend on the offending article or individual, re-tweeting their outrage in the most abusive terms while demanding an apology/retraction/public execution. Notable examples of such Twitch-hunts include the mass hounding of *Daily Mail* journalist Jan Moir (led by celebrity Twitterati), for criticising what she claimed was the gay lifestyle after the death of singer Stephen Gateley in October 2009; and the collective slating of comedian Alan Davies in April 2012, after he used his football podcast to question in insensitive terms Liverpool Football Club's refusal to play matches on the anniversary of the Hillsborough disaster. Both of these indiscretions were treated by outraged tweeters as if the perpetrators of the words had been urinating on the graves of the victims.

We are faced with a caricature of debate where some will tweet in a deliberately offensive style to get a reaction, and many more are just waiting to be outraged and offended so that they can start another Twitch-hunt. Meanwhile thin-skinned celebrities and tweeters forward offensive material directly to the police (who are also Twitter regulars these days), demanding legal action against the "trolls".

Toxic trolls versus the illiberal Twitter Taliban; if this is the free speech party, then who needs state repression? The atmosphere of conformism and closed minds in what ought to be the open spaces of the internet fringe looks like a depressing symptom of how far the cleansing of the media has already gone.

The "Despotism of Custom"

Who cares what happens to the tabloids? Why does all this matter, even if you hate the redtop papers and would never dream of reading them? It should matter to us all, because conformism is the anaesthetised death of freedom of thought and speech. It matters not a jot that those now supporting the "ethical" cleansing of the press do so from the moral and intellectual high ground, looking down on the misdeeds of the tabloid "lowlife". However worthy the cause in whose name it is enforced, a culture of conformism always has the effect of diminishing all that it touches. It kills true free expression and the free spirit, to the diminution of our humanity as a whole.

If those high-minded individuals who would purge the press today care to see somebody of even more elevated intellect than them defend genuine tolerance and freedom of expression against well-mannered conformism, let them look to John Stuart Mill, one of the leading English philosophers of all time.

In his classic 1859 work, *On Liberty*, Mill establishes the standing of freedom of expression as a foundation of civilised society, and the importance of defending it even when society believes the opinion expressed to be entirely wrong; to do otherwise, says Mill, is to assume the "infallibility" of conventional opinions.

Most importantly for our argument here, Mill also establishes that the threat to liberty and the freedom of thought and expression comes not only from tyrannical laws. It comes most dangerously from "the despotism of custom" — aka conformism — which he says is "everywhere the standing hindrance to human advancement". Under this "tyranny of opinion", Mill argues, people risk losing the capacity to think for themselves:

> "The mind itself is bowed to the yoke: even in what people do for pleasure, conformity is the first thing thought of;... peculiarity of taste, eccentricity of conduct, are shunned equally with crimes: until by dint of not following their own nature, they have no nature to follow: their human capacities are withered and starved: they become incapable of any strong wishes or native pleasures, and are generally without... opinions [that are] properly their own. Now is this, or is it not, the desirable condition of human nature?"

Against the deadening sway of the "despotism of custom", Mill says, anybody who holds dear to liberty and a forward-looking society should tolerate diversity, individuality, even eccentricity of thought and behaviour. "Why then should tolerance," he demands, "as far as the public sentiment is concerned, extend only to tastes and modes of life which extort acquiescence by the multitude of their adherents?" And he is clear that the freedom to break from the "tyranny" of conformism cannot be reserved solely for those deemed of sufficient moral or mental "rank" in society.

If a stand was not made against the despotism of custom, Mill warned, society would reach a point where all "deviations" from conformity were considered "impious, immoral, even monstrous and contrary to nature". Around 150 years later, that is pretty much the way in which the "ethical" cleansers look upon much of the popular press today.[24]

It is in the spirit of J.S. Mill that we ought to oppose the creeping culture of media conformism. Not because we necessarily want to defend or celebrate the available alternatives, whether they be Page 3 pin-ups or celebrity scandal stories. But because we recognise that compulsory conformism kills a free press, free thinking and eventually a free society.

Diversity in the "Marketplace of Ideas"

Many would agree on the need to encourage greater diversity in all forms of the media. They generally focus on the problem of ownership, and the grip which a handful of big corporations exercise over the mainstream media. That situation is certainly regrettable and reinforces the closure of the media mind. The monopolisation of the media market has also long posed a problem for those attempting to break into it. I well recall the grim struggle of simply trying to get our small Left-wing magazines on to the shelves of WH Smith.

But the diversity we need above all else today is that of content and ideas and values. No matter who owns and publishes it, the media today is too much of a monotone, and it is becoming harder to tell a conformist liberal paper from a conformist conservative one. Instead of simply harping on about the problem of ownership, critics would do better to put those energies into trying to develop an alternative media — certainly a more constructive use of energies than joining in the crusade to purge the existing press and copper-bottom the culture of conformism.

There is a problem here that the tabloid-bashers and Murdochphobics tend to avoid; that the reason the media holds such sway is not merely down to monopoly ownership, far less to any stupidity of the mass of readers. It is because of the historical failure of the left and other movements in society to build popular support for any alternative newspapers or other alternative media. The shrill harping on about Murdoch and the media empires often looks like whistling past the graveyard, an attempt to avoid facing up to that awkward truth.

Despite the size and influence of the media monopolies, there is more opportunity to try to create an alternative voice today. The internet has broken down many of the barriers that kept different viewpoints out of the media "marketplace of ideas". There are chances now to encourage a more open, diverse, eccentric and above all non-conformist online media in every direction. Our efforts would be far better spent in that project than in demanding that Lord Justice Leveson or anybody else in authority somehow liberate the press by purging it.

The trouble is that in today's atmosphere even the demand for greater media diversity can turn into a recipe for further conformism. One of the main campaigns for press regulation post-hacking, a collection of activists and academics called the Coordinating Committee for Media Reform, wants to encourage greater diversity of media ownership through public funding for alternative publications. Even leaving aside the unlikelihood of acquiring such cash hand-outs in these straitened times, could anything seem more guaranteed to crush the spirit of new voices in the media than making them submit applications for state funding? That sort of official "diversity" always involves ticking enough boxes to prove you meet the ethical and possibly ethnic standards required. The result, as seen across the publicly-funded cultural sphere, is greater politically and emotionally correct conformism, enforced in the name of diversity.

What we need is more openness in the media—to new publications, new ideas, new forms of entertainment. We need a spirit of true tolerance, where no voice is barred from being heard, and of genuine judgementalism, where nobody is allowed to get away with anything unchallenged. We need the freedom to think for ourselves and the open-mindedness to let others do the same.

What we don't need is the mission to purge the press and "ethically" cleanse the mass media in all of its forms, whether that mission is pursued by Lord Justice Leveson or a collective of Twitterati. Everything about that mission, from the posturing against "underhand and unethical" reporting methods to the insistence that only their definition of "public interest journalism" deserves press freedom, will contribute to a narrower, duller and tamer press. Those who dream of helping Leveson and the government to create a sanitised media in an "ideal world" should be reminded at every turn that in the real world a free press is indivisible.

The struggle for press freedom in Britain began more than five hundred years ago as a fight for the right to depart from religious orthodoxy and express non-conformist beliefs. How did conformism to a new secular orthodoxy, the scourge of a free press, ever become the demand of those campaigning for media reform today?

1   Michael Gove at the Leveson Inquiry, 29 May 2012 (http://www.levesoninquiry.org.uk/wp-content/uploads/2012/05/Transcript-of-Afternoon-Hearing-29-May-2012.txt).
2   Quoted in *The Times*, 27 January 2012.
3   See Mick Hume, 'Some last thoughts on that libel trial', *Spiked*, 24 May 2001 (http://www.spiked-online.com/Articles/00000002D0E3.htm).
4   The *Guardian*, 24 April 2012.
5   George Orwell, *The Freedom of the Press*, 1945.
6   The *Guardian*, 31 May 2012.
7   Jackie Ashley, the *Guardian*, 30 April 2012.
8   The *Guardian*, 18 November 2011.
9   *The Times*, 26 November 2011.
10 The *Guardian*, 26 November 2011.
11 Henry Porter, *The Observer*, 27 November 2011.
12 Ian Hislop at the Leveson Inquiry, 17 January 2012 (http://www.Levesoninquiry.org.uk/wp-content/uploads/2012/01/Transcript-of-Morning-Hearing-17-January-2012.pdf).
13 James Harding at the Leveson Inquiry, 17 January 2012, *ibid.*
14 The *Guardian*, 9 July 2012.
15 *The Times*, 31 March 2012.
16 Quoted in Journalism.co.uk, 6 February 2012.

[17] See Patrick Hayes, 'A licence to kill freedom of expression', *Spiked*, 5 October 2011 (http://www.spiked-online.com/site/article/11141/).

[18] Reprinted in the *Guardian*, 11 September 2011.

[19] *Newsnight*, BBC2, 26 March 2012.

[20] The *Guardian*, 19 February 2012.

[21] See Frank Furedi, *On Tolerance: A Defence of Moral Independence*, Continuum 2011, p. 201.

[22] Quoted in James Boswell, *The Life of Samuel Johnson*, Everyman's Library Classics 1992, p. 744.

[23] Quoted in *Media Guardian*, 22 March 2012.

[24] John Stuart Mill, *On Liberty*, Chapter 3, pp. 68, 78.

Chapter Seven

Manifesto for a Free Press

There is no such thing as a free press today. And we need one more than ever.

For all the reasons discussed in this book the British press is neither free nor open enough—even before the tough new regulator comes into force. External pressures and internal problems have already put journalism under stress. The phone-hacking scandal has now become the pretext for purging the press, the Leveson Inquiry into press culture and ethics acting as an inquisition on a mission to instil a new culture of conformism. Whatever the problems of the press, these responses can only make worse the absence of freedom, open-mindedness and plurality in the UK media today.

This at a time when, in the midst of a social and economic crisis and the demise of the old politics, there has never been a greater need for a full and open public debate about which way we want our society, politics and economy to go in the future.

There is a chance for the press in all its forms to become part of the possible solution rather than being blamed for all of the problems all of the time—especially with the opportunities offered by the new media. Which makes it worse still that in this hour of need and opportunity, the media is so stymied and conformist—and will become more so, if those pushing for the purging of the press have their way.

So, what is to be done about the press? We need to address these issues in the broadest form, to incorporate not only

traditional newspapers but the new frontiers of online publications in all shapes and sizes too.

Yes, what is needed is a change in the culture of the press —
but more importantly still, a drastic change in cultural attitudes
towards the press. And not a culture change to be somehow
imposed by the wave of a hand from a judge or a government
minister.

We need to start by turning the assumptions of the current
debate about press regulation on their head. The problem is not
that the UK press has too much freedom to run wild, but too
little liberty. The trouble is not that the UK press is too far out-
of-control, but that it is far too conformist.

The danger is not that press freedom in the UK is too open
to abuse, but that the British press and media are not open
enough, too closed off from a free exchange of thought; not
simply that the press is too tied to the market, but that it is too
hidebound to allow access to the "marketplace of ideas".

A few thoughts follow on the sort of things worth standing
for to begin to address the problem. Some are specific proposals.
Most are about the need, not for new laws, but for a cultural
revolution in the way we view press freedom today.

- Freedom of expression is nobody's gift. Everybody says they
  support press freedom — then most attach a "But…" to say
  how it should be limited, at least for others. A free press has
  to mean just that — free, for everybody who wishes to use or
  even to abuse that freedom. Press freedom is not divisible, or
  a gift to be rationed out by judges or governments to those
  deemed worthy of it. You cannot abolish slavery, but only
  for white people. And you cannot have press freedom for
  the quality media but not for the popular. We need to stand
  for a free press, with no ifs or "Buts…", warts and all. As the
  young Karl Marx said of a free press 170 years ago, "You
  cannot pluck the rose without its thorns!" A free press
  requires diversity and plurality, not the imposition of orthodoxy or a single "public taste". An untamed and dirty free
  press will always better than a cleaned-up conformist one if
  we hope for a clash that can get us closer to the truth.

- No to the "ethical" cleansing of the media. The demand for ethical journalism around the Leveson Inquiry might seem a no-brainer. Who could be in favour of "unethical journalism"? But ethical rules do not come out of the ether. They are a code for expressing a particular agenda in specific circumstances. Today, the demand to protect "ethical" journalism and trash the rest is a divisive recipe for disaster. Ethics has become the shield behind which media snobs seek to purge the press of that which is not to their taste. Just as religious fundamentalists call on the authority of their God in support of their personal prejudices, so today's secular crusaders call down the might of other-worldly ethics to justify the imposition of their earthbound agendas and interests.

  Freedom is a messy business, and not everybody who chooses to exercise it will necessarily have the sanctity of Jesus, the high-mindedness of Lord Justice Leveson or the moral piety of Hugh Grant. That is no reason for purging heretics. For as John Wilkes, the eighteenth-century hero of the struggle for press freedom and a scoundrel, liar and pornographer declared on the front page of the newspaper which he was sent to the Tower for publishing: the "liberty of the press" is the "birthright of every Briton" — and anybody else in our society.

  Resisting the attempt at "ethical" cleansing is not about upholding "unethical" journalism. It is about defending freedom, a free and open press for all and not just for those sanctioned by social worthies. It is about recognising that the elitist campaign to purge the popular press is really designed to curb the tastes and passions of the populace. Either we have a free press or we do not. And there is no need to fantasise about Britain becoming Zimbabwe-on-Sea in order to see that ours is not nearly free or open enough.

- Publish, and be judged — by the public, not the judges. Everybody says that what we need is "public interest journalism". And who could be against that? But the purified notion of the "public interest" is as loaded as that of "ethical journalism". Who is to decide what is in the public interest to publish? Lord Justice Leveson and his bewigged and learned, but unelected and unaccountable, friends on the judges' bench? Simon Cowell and David Walliams? Or should we revive the British tradition of the licensing of the press by the Crown, and have her majesty the Queen decide, perhaps assisted by celebrity Princess Kate?

In a free society only the public can decide what is in its interests — or, which is equally legitimate, simply what interests it. And it can only decide once everything is out there in the public arena. Whether the issue is leaked government documents or celebrity gossip, the principle should be to publish first, and let the audience ask questions and judge for themselves later. The Duke of Wellington famously challenged his detractors in the press to "Publish, and be damned!" Today the only challenge facing the press should be to have the courage to publish what it believes to be true and be judged by the public — while the judges and officials stay out of it.

- Better fewer laws, but better. The notion that there are not enough legally-enforceable restraints on the UK media is a bizarre distortion of the truth. The British press is hemmed in and harassed on all sides by dozens of laws, and the list is growing. We need to get the state's nose out of the newspapers and other media. The press has to be subject to the same system of criminal justice as everybody else. But no more than that. There should be no laws that single out the press for special treatment or criminalise free speech and the normal business of investigative journalism. Nor should we accept, far less encourage, any police fishing expeditions targeting journalists and editors. Any and all burdensome legal impediments to a free press should be opposed in the spirit of the First Amendment to the US Constitution, which declares that government "shall pass no law abridging the freedom of speech, or of the press".

- Libel laws are a crime against liberty. Everybody with a liberal bone in their body recognises that English defamation laws are the worst in the civilised world and a disgrace to democracy. A top US court called them "repugnant" to the principle of free speech, and that is putting it politely. (I held these views long before I was sued for libel, forced to close the independent magazine I edited and left a million quid in debt...)

But while many respectable figures campaign for libel law reform these days, there is a tendency both to over- and under-estimate the scale of the problem. They overestimate the problem by talking as if libel law was the sole or even the major barrier to freedom of expression today. It is not; it is simply the odious legal arm of a broader and deeper cultural hostility to free speech and a free press, which it both feeds off and supplements. And they tend to underestimate the problem by calling for reforms that would leave intact the central iniquity of the libel laws as a crime against the liberty of the press. Indeed in welcoming proposals to leave more libel cases to a judge rather than a jury, some reformers risk reinforcing the elitist, illiberal character of the law. As defenders of a free press we would do better to revive and update the spirit of Cato, the eighteenth-century newspaper essayist, who declared that "I would rather many libels escape than there be any restrictions on a free press".

- For true Tolerance and genuine Judgementalism. The debate about a free press and freedom of expression is marred by twin ills. One on hand there is a creeping intolerance of anything deemed "offensive", and an attempt to ban or curtail it in the name of tolerance; as London mayor Boris Johnson put it in banning Christian bus adverts about homosexuality, we are now supposed to be "intolerant of intolerance". On the other hand, there is a cult of non-judgementalism that says some things ought to be beyond question or immune from "disrespectful" and "offensive" criticism. The net result of these trends is to reinforce the culture of You Can't Say That in the media and beyond. We need to counter them both.

True tolerance means allowing others the freedom to say and publish things that you don't want to hear. Genuine judgementalism means having the liberty to tell them exactly what you think of it. The first response to any controversy should be: You Can Say That. Just so long as you take responsibility for your words, and we can then say you are talking bunk; or even tell you that you shouldn't have said it, just because you can. Our best weapons in striving for the truth are scepticism and argument, not sanctimony and intolerance. Let the motto of a free press be "Ban Nothing—Question Everything".

- For self-regulation—with the emphasis on self, not regulation. The Leveson Inquiry has revealed a worrying consensus in favour of more regulation of the press. Whether the proposals are for a state-backed "independent" regulator, or "self-regulation" by a new body with greater powers to police the press than are currently enjoyed by the police, all of the different plans rest on the assumption that what the media reports needs to be more tightly regulated. Why? Stricter press regulation won't deal with an individual crime such as phone-hacking. It will, however, put the entire press under house arrest. Never mind the "yes to press freedom, But…" lobby. It is a contradiction to try to support both a free press and tighter external regulation in whatever state-backed, "independent" or other form.

What the media needs is a sense of greater liberty to report on and publish what it sees fit and believes to be true. Of course there must be agreed basic standards and rules; for example the press could enhance its cause if it took simple steps to correct wrong information and allegations against individuals more swiftly and prominently. But the last thing our press needs is to be looking over its shoulder for yet another policeman in plain clothes.

- We need a public life, not privacy laws. The hysteria about press intrusion into private lives is a bad case of shooting the messenger. The media is largely reflecting and reinforcing a culture where exhibitionism and voyeurism have become social norms and everybody from the government downwards has lost a clear sense of where the line might be between the public and private spheres. What we need is not yet another law or more court injunctions to limit what can be reported, but an open debate about the proper role of society's public life, and the importance of a separate private sphere.

The best way to defend privacy would be actually to create a healthy political and public sphere. One where it is acknowledged that it is no business of politicians and state officials to meddle in people's private affairs and tell us how to eat, parent or live—and no interest of ours to judge public figures on their private affairs. Recreating a proper sense of the public provides the best chance of instilling respect for a discrete private sphere. But that will take another major cultural shift, not just a new law. A privacy law that further curtails public discussion is that last thing we require to defend the private sphere.

- Underhand does not necessarily mean beneath contempt. The phone-hacking scandal has become a pretext for interrogating and condemning all manner of investigative tools and reporting methods. It seems that anything which appears underhand can now be branded "unethical", if not illegal, from "blagging" information or paying for it to going through bin bags or making secret recordings. If this continues it will spell the end of proper investigative reporting —an endangered species of news even now.

Investigative journalism is about trying to elicit information that somebody else—often somebody in a position of power—does not want you to obtain, far less publish. That necessarily involves using underhand and sometimes questionable methods. In deciding whether these are justified, each case must be weighed on its merits. Journalists must be allowed to make judgement calls and then judged accordingly, rather than condemned in advance for infringing some general code of ethics delivered from the heavens. Even phone-hacking has been justified on occasion by the upper end of the media. As for obtaining information from police and public officials, that is part of the lifeblood of reporters. Public institutions should of course have proced-ures in place for protecting their information and disciplin-ing staff who betray confidences. But don't blame the press for striving to get round those procedures and get the story.

- For investigative journalism, not voyeurism. The problem that exploded the phone-hacking scandal was not simply the methods the *News of the World* used—it was some of the tar-gets they chose and the motives for doing so. Hacking into the voicemail messages of an abducted teenager was not journalism, it was voyeurism. It is important to say that should have no place in news reporting.

    But it is also worth saying that the *NotW* and the tabloid press have not had a monopoly on voyeurism masquerad-ing as journalism. The upmarket media might pick their targets more tastefully. But rooting through and publishing Syrian president Assad's lovey-dovey emails to his wife, or Wikileaks-type revelations about world leaders' personal proclivities, or even micro-examining David Cameron's LOL text messages to Rebekah Brooks, are no more investigative journalism than hacking crime victims' phones. It is high-end voyeurism for middle class punters. It would be a start if more media outlets could devote the sort of energy to investigative reporting deployed by the late and largely unlamented *News of the World*, in pursuit of their own stories.

- Down with Twitch-hunts and troll-hounding. The open spaces of the internet ought to provide our best hope for the future of a free press. The trouble is that they are becoming infected with the creeping thin-skinned culture of You Can't Say That from the mainstream media. The social networking and information-sharing site Twitter, hailed by its UK front-man as "the free speech wing of the free speech party", has also become the provisional wing of the Intolerant Tolerance movement. Anything deemed too offensive—especially from a journalist—is likely to spark an abusive Twitter-mob or mass "Twitch-hunt" against the author, a thought-policing exercise possibly including being reported to the actual police. Internet "trolls" who fire bitter online abuse at celebrities and others have been targeted in the press and become the subject of high-profile crackdowns.

We cannot allow the wilder corners of internet to be colonised by militant conformists in this fashion. Twitch-hunts are not "democracy in action", they're only a fashionable incarnation of the creeping elitist contempt for freedom of expression. Public troll-hounding is a waste of energy that can only confirm the trolls in their mission and reaffirm the message that there are things which cannot be said. No doubt there are many sick and deeply offensive things being vomited onto the internet. So what? Better by far to encourage an attitude of ignoring the nonsense on Twitter and the web. Let the twits twitter. There is no point trying to stop it, far less to persecute or sue it. The freedom of the web is far too important to be sacrificed to catch irritating flies.

- For a serious grounded journalism amid the online free-for-all. The right response to the anything-goes, sometimes poisonous, atmosphere on the wilder parts of the web is not to try to tame it or sue it for defamation. It is surely to focus on ensuring we have a serious, grounded counter-weight of proper, professional journalism. Maintaining a school of journalism that can distinguish facts from feelings, that sees the truth as something that you have to strive for rather than assume, and that puts objective investigation ahead of subjective emotions or invective is more necessary in the current atmosphere of promiscuous abuse-hurling. Perhaps above all, in all forms of the future press we are going to require a journalism that is open-minded enough to counter the closing down of serious debate. The old *Guardian* editor C.P. Scott famously stated the journalistic ethos that "Comment is free but facts are sacred". Too often today we seem faced with a situation where comment and opinion are far from "free", while the sacred status of facts can be sacrificed on the altar of a cause or a crusade. A free press needs both to stick to the facts, and to let a thousand ideas and opinions bloom.

- Journalism as an open calling, not a closed profession. In the clamour to reform and "clean up" the press in the wake of the phone-hacking scandal, there have been proposals from within the industry and especially from media academics to turn journalism into more of a controlled profession, by emulating the model of medicine or the law and even by licensing journalists. Some suggest that the press could then self-regulate along similar lines to those professions, including measures to debar or "strike off" journalists who do not meet the standards laid down from above. These ideas might be well-intentioned, but they risk striking a serious blow against press freedom.

  Journalism is no more than the paid — and increasingly the unpaid — exercise of the general right to freedom of expression. That is why it should be open to anybody who feels called to it or simply has something to say. High-level journalism is already too much of a closed shop for the well-connected and privately-educated so far as most would-be writers are concerned. It should not be treated as a closed profession requiring special entry standards and regulations. Journalists are not doctors or lawyers (as a glance at the pay slips of most struggling hacks would readily confirm). A system allowing them to be "struck off" or denied a press card for breaching some enforced code would be anathema to press freedom, a new form of licensing the media and controlling who is allowed to report. Professional journalism, in terms of standards and seriousness, always; but journalism as a closed profession, never.

- Ownership: whose press is it anyway? Critics of the current state of the press in the UK and elsewhere in the West often focus, sometimes obsessively, on the issue of media ownership. The increasing concentration of print and broadcasting outlets in the hands of a few huge media corporations is blamed not only for the problems of the press, but also it seems for the problems of society and the planet.

The concentration of press ownership in media conglomerates is certainly nothing to celebrate. It has often proved an impediment to the exercise of a free press. Nobody who wants to see diversity in the media could welcome this state of affairs. There is, however, another side to this problem that the radical critics are less keen to focus on: the failure of any alternative newspapers and media outlets to sustain a serious audience. It is no good blaming either the "gullible" punters and "sheeple", or even Rupert Murdoch, for the inability to make an alternative press flourish.

Short of an anti-capitalist revolution, it is hard to envisage any miraculous democratisation of mainstream media ownership in the UK or the US. So what is the alternative? We will not know unless we try. If the energy devoted to attacking the media moguls, and the hope invested in Lord Justice Leveson to rout the demon press barons, was instead concentrated on developing ideas and investment for an alternative media, the future of the free press in all its forms would look far rosier.

- Seize the day for a free press. It seems strange that there should be so much doom and gloom about the state of the media and the future of the press, at a time when we are presented with an historic opportunity to forge something fresh through the internet. The traditional newspaper industry is clearly in decline—though ironically it exercises more influence than ever over our shrivelled public and political life. Yet there are opportunities that have never existed since the arrival of the printing press to reach new audiences with new forms of media online, without the upfront costs associated with printing. Of course nobody can expect easily to displace the mainstream media. But it would be a start if people who want to see something different could stop obsessing about Murdoch, or asking the likes of Lord Justice Leveson to solve all of our problems, and instead focus on generating new ideas and good journalism, and creating alternatives. The future of a free, open and pluralistic press in all its forms is yet to be written.

- Conformism is the enemy. What is needed most in the media today is a diversity, not merely of ownership or of ethnic and class backgrounds, but of opinions, voices and viewpoints. Conformism is the greatest enemy of press freedom in a society such as Britain. It is what makes censorship unnecessary, and open debate impossible. Measures to police media ownership would not address the conformity of content. Imposing a culture of conformism through the "ethical" cleansing of the press has been the mission of the Leveson inquisition and its many supporters. The first fighters for a free press in sixteenth- and seventeenth-century England did it in order to express their non-conformist religious views. We need to revive that spirit of non-conformism in these secular times.

- Yes to righting serious wrongs — no to a right to reply. There are some simple steps the press could take to counter the hostile public perceptions generated around the phone-hacking scandal and Leveson Inquiry. One such would be to deal with the constant complaint that newspapers refuse to publish corrections and apologies when individuals are wrongly accused or defamed — or that they hide away corrections to prominent articles. This sore issue has been exploited by those who want to see more press regulation. They demand the creation of a media ombudsman with the power to force the publication of corrections and apologies; or a system of prior notice whereby the press would have to inform anybody they intended publishing a story about, who could then ask a judge to stop it; or even a legally enforceable "right to reply", guaranteeing the wronged party a response to be published as prominently as the original story.

  Any of these impositions would represent a serious blow to the freedom of the press to investigate and publish as it sees fit. Nobody who cares about a free press would want to see it effectively edited by unaccountable ombudsmen or judges, or clogged with lengthy self-serving responses from upset celebrities or politicians and their PR advisors. A more satisfactory solution would be for the press itself to move quickly to set up its own measures for the rapid and reasonable publication of corrections, retractions and apologies — where serious mistakes and misjudgements are made that damage people, not every time some self-important figure says their feelings have been hurt. The advent of publication online should allow the flexibility to make this happen more readily. Some publications have already taken steps in this direction with the appointment of readers' editors. That might not be ideal but seems preferable to the imposition of outside editorial control in name of the readers.

- Dine with whoever has the story — but take a long spoon. The backlash against the close relations between the authorities and the press in recent times has reached a pitch where it seems some would be happy if no journalist ever spoke to or had a drink with a politician or a policeman again. In reality such contacts are a vital part of reporters' work. What free journalists need to remember is that when you dine with the elites, it is best to take a long spoon.

  The press has become a central part of a closed media-political class, exercising great influence over public life as the authority of other institutions from parliament to political parties has withered. Carried away with its own importance, the press has too often acted as part of an insulated oligarchy atop society, taking on roles which are outside its proper function. Instead we need a more independent, open-minded media that can play its part in the sort of public debate required to revitalise political life.

- No to narcissism. The central role that the media occupies in our public life today has come about largely through default, as the authority of other institutions from political parties and churches to parliament and trade unions has withered. Nevertheless the increased influence of the press has encouraged the scourge of narcissism and delusions of grandeur in the media. Self-important sections of the press have sometimes imagined themselves in roles ranging from the "real" opposition to elected governments to the saviours of the wretched of the Earth and the planet itself. Journalists and media outlets have sometimes acted less as objective reporters and more like self-righteous crusaders on a one-eyed mission to vanquish their chosen evil, be that "paedos" at home or "Nazis" abroad.

The hacking of innocent victims' phones was a symptom of the culture of narcissism that made some think they could do anything in pursuit of a cause they deemed righteous. The hysteria that treated those historical cases of phone-hacking as the most important story around is another symptom of the narcissism that means anything to do with the media becomes the biggest news. A free press is reliant on the work of campaigning journalists. Narcissistic crus-aders it can do without.

- Journalism should be more humble—and take itself more seriously. We need journalism to show a little more humility and recognise that its primary responsibility is to report and reflect the world, not to run it or rescue it. Yet at the same time, journalism should take itself more seriously and recog-nise just how important it is. A free media has a vital role to play in informing public debate with the facts and the argu-ments that society needs to get close to the truth and to move forwards. It is far too important to be reduced to an effusion of journalists' feelings or the reproduction of some-body else's PR fluff or shallow tweets. It might not be the job of journalists to save the planet or tell people how to live. But it is their responsibility to tell it like it is.

- Defend the right of a free press to be a mess. Freedom is always a messy affair, as people take advantage of it in their own chosen fashion. That freedom is something to be celeb-rated, not curtailed or "cleaned up". The raucous, insolent and often offensive voices of the media are the sound of liberty. And the much-maligned "popular" press is as much a vital part of that free media as the highest-minded broad-sheet or the most public-spirited BBC programme. Defend the right to be "popular", and recognise that attacks on the tabloid press have long been a backhanded way of expressing contempt for the populace. By all means let us take the press to task for all of its problems and perfidies. But let's also defend the right of a free press to be an unwieldy mess, and resist all attempts to sanitise, disinfest, shrink-wrap or otherwise make safe and respectable a press that was born in the flames of controversy and will always be making and getting into trouble while it lives and breathes.